# Start∪p

Ken Beatty, Series Consultant

6

Jenifer Edens
Steve Gwynne
Linda L. Lane
Don Linder
Daria Ruzicka
Jenni Currie Santamaria
Randa Taftaf
Geneva Tesh

MW01042267

**StartUp 6**

Pearson, 221 River Street, Hoboken, NJ 07030

**Staff credits:** The people who made up the StartUp team representing editorial, production, and design are Pietro Alongi, Héctor González Álvarez, Gregory Bartz, Peter Benson, Magdalena Berkowska, Stephanie Callahan, Jennifer Castro, Tracey Munz Cataldo, Dave Dickey, Gina DiLillo, Irene Frankel, Sarah Henrich, Christopher Leonowicz, Bridget McLaughlin, Kamila Michalak, Laurie Neaman, Alison Pei, Jennifer Raspiller, Jeremy Schaar, Katherine Sullivan, Stephanie Thornton, Paula Van Ells, and Joseph Vella.

**Cover credit:** Front cover: Javier Osores/EyeEm/Getty Images. Back cover: Klaus Vedfelt/Getty Images (Level 1); Alexandre Moreau/Getty Images (Level 2); Matteo Colombo/Getty Images (Level 3); Javier Osores/EyeEm/Getty Images (Level 4); Liyao Xie/Getty Images (Level 5); Ezra Bailey/Getty Images (Level 6); guvendemir/Getty Images (Level 7); Yusuke Shimazu/EyeEm/Getty Images (Level 8); tovovan/Shutterstock (icons)

**Text composition:** emc design ltd

Library of Congress cataloging-in-publication data on file.

**Photo and illustration credits:** See pages 166–167

Printed in the United States of America

ISBN-10: 0-13-468420-6

ISBN-13: 978-0-13-468420-8

ISBN-10: 0-13-517841-X (with app and Online Practice)

ISBN-13: 978-0-13-517841-6 (with app and Online Practice)

1 2019

# ACKNOWLEDGMENTS

We would like to thank the following people for their insightful and helpful comments and suggestions.

**Maria Alam**, Extension Program-Escuela Americana, San Salvador, El Salvador; **Milton Ascencio**, Universidad Don Bosco, Soyapango, El Salvador; **Raul Avalos**, CALUSAC, Guatemala City, Guatemala; **Adrian Barnes**, Instituto Chileno Norteericano, Santiago, Chile; **Laura Bello**, Centro de Idiomas Xalapa, Universidad Veracruzana, Xalapa, México; **Jeisson Alonso Rodriguez Bonces**, Fort Dorchester High School, Bogotá, Colombia; **Juan Pablo Calderón Bravo**, Manpower English, Santiago, Chile; **Ellen J. Campbell**, RMIT, Ho Chi Minh City, Vietnam; **Vinicio Cancinos**, CALUSAC, Guatemala City, Guatemala; **Viviana Castilla**, Centro de Enseñanza de Lenguas Extranjeras UN, México; **Bernal Cespedes**, ULACIT, Tournón, Costa Rica; **Carlos Celis**, Cel. Lep Idiomas S.A., São Paulo, Brazil; **Carlos Eduardo Aguilar Cortes**, Universidad de los Andes, Bogotá, Colombia; **Solange Lopes Vinagre Costa**, Senac-SP, São Paulo, Brazil; **Isabel Cubilla**, Panama Bilingüe, Panama City, Panama; **Victoria Dieste**, Alianza Cultural Uruguay-Estados Unidos, Montevideo, Uruguay; **Francisco Domerque**, Georgal Idiomas, México City, México; **Vern Eaton**, St. Giles International, Vancouver, Canada; **Maria Fajardo**, Extension Program-Escuela Americana, San Salvador, El Salvador; **Diana Elizabeth Leal Ffrench**, Let's Speak English, Cancún, México; **Rosario Giraldez**, Alianza Cultural Uruguay-Estados Unidos, Montevideo, Uruguay; **Lourdes Patricia Rodríguez Gómez**, Instituto Tecnológico de Chihuahua, Chihuahua, México; **Elva Elizabeth Martínez de González**, Extension Program-Escuela Americana, San Salvador, El Salvador; **Gabriela Guel**, Centro de Idiomas de la Normal Superior, Monterrey, México; **Ana Raquel Fiorani Horta**, SENAC, Ribeirão Preto, Brazil; **Carol Hutchinson**, Heartland International English School, Winnipeg, Canada; **Deyanira Solís Juárez**, Centro de Idiomas de la Normal Superior, Monterrey, México; **Miriam de Käppel**, Colegio Bilingüe El Prado, Guatemala City, Guatemala; **Ikuko Kashiwabara**, Osaka Electro-Communication University, Neyagawa, Japan; **Steve Kirk**, Nippon Medical School, Tokyo, Japan; **Jill Landry**, GEOS Languages Plus, Ottawa, Canada; **Tiffany MacDonald**, East Coast School of Languages, Halifax, Canada; **Angélica Chávez Escobar Martínez**, Universidad de León, León, Guanajuato, México; **Renata Martinez**, CALUSAC, Guatemala City, Guatemala; **Maria Alejandra Mora**, Keiser International Language Institute, San Marcos, Carazo, Nicaragua; **Alexander Chapetón Morales**, Abraham Lincoln School, Bogotá, Colombia; **José Luis Castro Moreno**, Universidad de León, León, Guanajuato, México; **Yukari Naganuma**, Eikyojuku for English Teachers, Tokyo, Japan; **Erina Ogawa**, Daito Bunka University, Tokyo, Japan; **Carolina Zepeda Ortega**, Let's Speak English, Cancún, México; **Lynn Passmore**, Vancouver International College, Vancouver, Canada; **Noelle Peach**, EC English, Vancouver, Canada; **Ana-Marija Petrunic**, George Brown College, Toronto, Canada; **Romina Planas**, Centro Cultural Paraguayo Americano, Asunción, Paraguay; **Sara Elizabeth Portela**, Centro Cultural Paraguayo Americano, Asunción, Paraguay; **Luz Rey**, Centro Colombo Americano, Bogotá, Colombia; **Ana Carolina González Ramírez**, Universidad de Costa Rica, San José, Costa Rica; **Octavio Garduno Ruiz**, AIPT Service S.C., Coyoacán, México; **Amado Sacalxot**, Colegio Lehnsen Americas, Guatemala City, Guatemala; **Deyvis Sanchez**, Instituto Cultural Dominico-Americano, Santo Domingo, Dominican Republic; **Lucy Slon**, JFK Adult Centre, Montreal, Canada; **Scott Stulberg**, University of Regina, Regina, Canada; **Maria Teresa Suarez**, Colegios APCE, San Salvador, El Salvador; **Daniel Valderrama**, Centro Colombo Americano, Bogotá, Colombia; **Kris Vicca**, Feng Chia University, Taichung, Taiwan; **Sairy Matos Villanueva**, Centro de Actualización del Magisterio, Chetumal, Q.R., México; **Edith Espino Villarreal**, Universidad Tecnológica de Panama, El Dorado, Panama; **Isabela Villas Boas**, Casa Thomas Jefferson, Brasília, Brazil

# LEARNING OBJECTIVES

## WELCOME UNIT

**page 2**  In the classroom | Learn about your book | Learn about your app

| Unit | Vocabulary | Grammar | Conversation / Speaking | Listening |
|---|---|---|---|---|
| **1**<br><br>**What have you been watching?**<br><br>**page 5** | • Ways to describe movies or TV shows<br>• Elements of a movie or TV show | • Present perfect continuous: Review and expand<br>• *What* clauses for emphasis<br>• *By* to explain how | • Describe what you've been watching<br>• Summarize the plot of a movie or TV show<br>• Discuss great movies<br><br>**Skill** Express degrees of enthusiasm | • Listen to a talk about great movies<br><br>**Skill** Listen for examples |
| **2**<br><br>**What's your return policy?**<br><br>**page 17** | • Return policy language<br>• Language for loans | • *As long as, providing (that), unless*<br>• Past unreal conditional<br>• Connectives to express contrast and surprise | • Ask about a return policy<br>• Discuss taking out a loan<br>• Talk about crowdfunding<br><br>**Skill** Ask questions for clarification | • Listen to a talk about crowdfunding<br><br>**Skill** Listen for the introduction and conclusion |
| **3**<br><br>**Have you seen a doctor?**<br><br>**page 29** | • Flu symptoms<br>• Injuries and treatments | • Giving and asking for advice: Review and expand<br>• Reporting advice: Review and expand<br>• *Not only…but also* | • Describe how you feel and ask for advice<br>• Describe injuries and report advice<br>• Talk about medical research<br><br>**Skill** Respond to bad news | • Listen to a talk about medical research<br><br>**Skill** Listen for topics |
| **4**<br><br>**Are you doing anything special?**<br><br>**page 41** | • Park rules<br>• Outdoor activities | • *Be supposed to*<br>• Future continuous<br>• Reduced restrictive relative clauses | • Talk about park rules<br>• Talk about outdoor activities<br>• Discuss how to help the environment<br><br>**Skill** Maintain a conversation by asking questions | • Listen to a talk about how to help the environment<br><br>**Skill** Listen for cause and effect |
| **5**<br><br>**What seems to be the problem?**<br><br>**page 53** | • Technology problems<br>• Technology solutions | • Past perfect continuous<br>• *Need* with gerunds and passive infinitives<br>• Infinitives as subject complements | • Describe technology problems<br>• Talk about technology solutions<br>• Discuss how technology affects us<br><br>**Skill** Reassure someone | • Listen to a talk about how technology affects us<br><br>**Skill** Listen for counterarguments |

| Pronunciation | Reading | Writing | Presentation |
|---|---|---|---|
| • *What* clauses | • Read about changes caused by technology<br><br>**Skill** Recognize jargon | • Write about a movie or TV show<br><br>**Skill** Write a strong topic sentence | • Give a presentation about your favorite kind of movie or TV show<br><br>**Skill** Stay calm |
| • Blend past modals | • Read about the health benefits of giving<br><br>**Skill** Identify sources of information | • Write an email to dispute a problem<br><br>**Skill** Use polite language in a formal email | • Give a presentation about an interesting crowdfunding project<br><br>**Skill** Speak with authority |
| • Link consonant and vowel sounds | • Read about the pros and cons of an issue<br><br>**Skill** Identify pros and cons | • Write a summary<br><br>**Skill** Write a good summary | • Give a presentation about an app or innovation that can improve people's health<br><br>**Skill** Keep graphics simple |
| • *Supposed to* | • Read a travel website<br><br>**Skill** Recognize hyperbole | • Write a persuasive argument<br><br>**Skill** Introduce opposing arguments | • Give a presentation about a beautiful natural place<br><br>**Skill** Give your audience an overview |
| • Link final consonants to beginning consonants | • Read an article about hacking<br><br>**Skill** Identify contrasts | • Write a product review<br><br>**Skill** Write relevant subheadings | • Give a presentation about an advance in technology<br><br>**Skill** Speak slowly and clearly |

| Unit | Vocabulary | Grammar | Conversation / Speaking | Listening |
|---|---|---|---|---|
| 6<br><br>Where was it made?<br><br>page 65 | • Materials and decorative objects<br>• Musical terms and descriptions | • Simple present and simple past passive: Review<br>• Restrictive and non-restrictive relative clauses: Review and expand<br>• *You, they, can / can't, could / couldn't* for general truths | • Describe a decorative object<br>• Describe music you like<br>• Discuss traditional food<br><br>Skill Express surprise | • Listen to a talk about traditional food<br><br>Skill Listen for supporting details |
| 7<br><br>When do you fly out?<br><br>page 77 | • Air travel terms<br>• Train and car travel terms | • Comparisons with gerund and noun phrases<br>• Past habits with *would / used to*: Review and expand<br>• *It* + past passive | • Talk about air travel preferences<br>• Talk about travel memories<br>• Discuss past transportation predictions<br><br>Skill Show strong agreement | • Listen to a talk about past transportation predictions<br><br>Skill Listen for adverbs of degree |
| 8<br><br>How have you been?<br><br>page 89 | • Ways of behaving<br>• Self-improvement language | • Modals for past regrets and possibilities<br>• *Wish* and *if only*: Review and expand<br>• Comparisons between clauses | • Talk about interacting with people<br>• Talk about self-improvement<br>• Discuss your bucket list<br><br>Skill Acknowledge a mistake | • Listen to a talk about bucket lists<br><br>Skill Listen for explanations |
| 9<br><br>Would you mind helping me?<br><br>page 101 | • Elements of the writing process<br>• Employment terms | • *Would / Do you mind* for permission and requests<br>• Modals with the passive<br>• *Likely* and *certain* + infinitive | • Ask for help and show appreciation<br>• Talk about possible changes at work<br>• Discuss ways to solve problems<br><br>Skill Express appreciation | • Listen to a talk about ways to solve problems<br><br>Skill Listen for tone and intended audience |
| 10<br><br>Has the city changed?<br><br>page 113 | • City features and changes<br>• Verbs for getting around | • *Do* or *did* for emphasis<br>• Past perfect with adverbial clauses of time: Review and expand<br>• Non-restrictive relative clauses for comments | • Talk about how cities change<br>• Talk about getting around a city<br>• Discuss lost and found items<br><br>Skill Introduce a popular opinion | • Listen to a talk about lost and found items<br><br>Skill Listen for attitude |

GRAMMAR PRACTICE / VOCABULARY PRACTICE .............. page 125

REFERENCES ......................................................... page 157

THE WRITING PROCESS ........................................ page 163

PRESENTATION SELF-EVALUATION ..................................... page 165

| Pronunciation | Reading | Writing | Presentation |
|---|---|---|---|
| • Pausing and intonation with relative clauses | • Read an article supporting a point of view<br><br>**Skill** Identify supporting reasons | • Write about how to do something<br><br>**Skill** Show the sequence of events | • Give a presentation about an interesting tradition<br><br>**Skill** Vary your intonation |
| • Reduced pronunciation of *than* | • Read about unique transportation systems<br><br>**Skill** Identify problems and solutions | • Write a thank-you email<br><br>**Skill** Choose the right level of formality | • Give a presentation about an interesting place<br><br>**Skill** Repeat your main ideas |
| • Link vowels within a word | • Read about overcoming rejection<br><br>**Skill** Notice transitions between paragraphs | • Write a narrative<br><br>**Skill** Use a variety of verb tenses | • Give a presentation about a goal you've achieved<br><br>**Skill** Sound conversational |
| • Intonation in lists | • Read about finding a job<br><br>**Skill** Emphasize ideas | • Write a letter of recommendation<br><br>**Skill** Use transition words and phrases to add information | • Give a presentation about your dream job<br><br>**Skill** Ignore distractions |
| • Emphasis of *do, does, did* | • Read about how a city has improved<br><br>**Skill** Make inferences | • Write about a favorite place<br><br>**Skill** Use a range of transition words to show comparison and contrast | • Give a presentation about a piece of public art<br><br>**Skill** Explain terms that may be new to the audience |

**Key**

▶ 00-00 audio      ▶ video      discussion      presentation self-evaluation

abc flashcards      ActiveTeach      web search

# TO THE TEACHER

## Welcome to *StartUp*

*StartUp* is an innovative eight-level, general American English course for adults and young adults who want to make their way in the world and need English to do it. The course takes students from CEFR A1 to C1 and enables teachers and students to track their progress in detail against the Global Scale of English (GSE) Learning Objectives.

| StartUp Level | GSE Range | CEFR | Description | StartUp Level | GSE Range | CEFR | Description |
|---|---|---|---|---|---|---|---|
| 1 | 22–33 | A1 | Beginner | 5 | 49–58 | B1+ | High intermediate |
| 2 | 30–37 | A2 | High beginner | 6 | 56–66 | B2 | Upper intermediate |
| 3 | 34–43 | A2+ | Low intermediate | 7 | 64–75 | B2+ | Low advanced |
| 4 | 41–51 | B1 | Intermediate | 8 | 73–84 | C1 | Advanced |

## English for 21st century learners

*StartUp* helps your students develop the spoken and written language they need to communicate in their personal, academic, and work lives. In each lesson, you help students build the collaborative and critical thinking skills so essential for success in the 21st century. *StartUp* allows students to learn the language in ways that work for them: anytime, anywhere. The Pearson Practice English App allows students to access their English practice on the go. Additionally, students have all the audio and video files at their fingertips in the app and on the Pearson English Portal.

## Personalized, flexible teaching

The unit structure and the wealth of support materials give you options to personalize the class to best meet your students' needs. *StartUp* gives you the freedom to focus on different strands and skills; for example, you can spend more class time on listening and speaking. You can choose to teach traditionally or flip the learning. You can teach sections of the lesson in the order you prefer. And you can use the ideas in the Teacher's Edition to help you extend and differentiate instruction, particularly for mixed-ability and for large and small classes.

## Motivating and relevant learning

*StartUp* creates an immersive learning experience with a rich blend of multimedia and interactive activities, including interactive flashcards for vocabulary practice; Grammar Coach and Pronunciation Coach videos; interactive grammar activities; podcasts, interviews, and other audio texts for listening practice; humorous, engaging videos with an international cast of characters for modeling conversations; high-interest video talks beginning at Level 5; media project videos in Levels 1–4 and presentation skills videos in Levels 5–6 for end-of-unit skills consolidation.

## Access at your fingertips

*StartUp* provides students with everything they need to extend their learning to their mobile device. The app empowers students to take charge of their learning outside of class, allowing them to practice English whenever and wherever they want, online or offline. The app provides practice of vocabulary, grammar, listening, and conversation. Students can go to any lesson by scanning a QR code on their Student Book page or through the app menu. The app also provides students with access to all the audio and video files from the course.

# Components

## For the Teacher

*StartUp* provides everything you need to plan, teach, monitor progress, and assess learning.

The *StartUp* **ActiveTeach** front-of-class tool allows you to

- zoom in on the page to focus the class's attention
- launch the vocabulary flashcard decks from the page
- use tools, like a highlighter, to emphasize specific text
- play all the audio texts and videos from the page
- pop up interactive grammar activities
- move easily to and from any cross-referenced pages

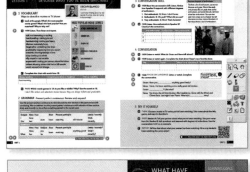

The interleaved **Teacher's Edition** includes

- an access code to the Pearson Practice English App and all digital resources
- language and culture notes
- teaching tips to help you improve your teaching practice
- *Look for* notes to help assess students' performance
- answer keys to all Student Book exercises on the facing page of the notes
- and more!

**Teacher's Digital Resources**, all available on the Pearson English Portal, include

- Teacher Methodology Handbook
- A unit walkthrough
- ActiveTeach front-of-class software
- ExamView assessment software
- Teacher's notes for every Student Book page
- Rubrics for speaking and writing
- Hundreds of reproducible worksheets
- Answer keys for all practice
- Audio and video scripts
- The GSE Teacher Mapping Booklet
- The GSE Toolkit

## For the Student

*StartUp* provides students with everything they need to extend their learning.

The optional **MyEnglishLab for *StartUp*** gives students more formal online practice and provides immediate feedback, hints, and tips. It includes

- grammar practice with remedial activities and access to all the Grammar Coach videos
- vocabulary practice, including games and flashcards
- speaking and pronunciation activities, including access to all the conversation videos and Pronunciation Coach videos
- listen-and-record practice that lets students record themselves and compare their recordings to models
- auto-graded reading and writing practice that reinforces skills taught in the Student Book
- summative assessments that measure students' mastery of listening, vocabulary, grammar, pronunciation, and reading
- a gradebook, which records scores on practice and assessments, that both students and you can use to help monitor progress and plan further practice

The optional *StartUp* **Workbook** provides practice of vocabulary, grammar, reading, and writing and includes self-assessments of grammar and vocabulary.

# WELCOME UNIT

## 1 IN THE CLASSROOM

**A** Get to know your classmates

Talk to your classmates. Find someone who matches each prompt. Write his or her first name on the line.

Find someone who...

- has received good news this month
  _____
- knows how they would spend $1 million
  _____
- had a hard time getting to class
  _____
- broke a bone when they were a child
  _____
- can recommend a funny TV show
  _____
- solved a technology problem this week
  _____

**B** Ask for help

▶00-01 Complete the conversations with sentences from the box. Then listen and check your answers.

| | |
|---|---|
| ~~Can you repeat the instructions?~~ | How do you pronounce this word? |
| What's the difference between "advice" and "advise"? | What's the English word for "barato"? |
| You're saying we should do this for homework? | Could you explain that a bit more? |

**1** Can you repeat the instructions?
Sure. Practice the conversation with a partner.
OK.

**2** Sorry—I still don't get it.
_____
Of course. Let me give you an example.

**3** Just to confirm—
_____
_____
That's right.
OK. Thanks.

**4** Can I ask you something?
_____
_____
The first word is a noun and the second is a verb.

**5** Can you remind me—
_____
_____
Cheap.
Oh, right. Thanks.

**6** _____
_____
Repeat after me: Gorgeous.
Gorgeous.
Correct.

**C** ROLE PLAY Choose a conversation from 1B. Make your own conversation. Use different information.

## 2 LEARN ABOUT YOUR BOOK

1. Look at pages iv-vii. What information is on those pages?

   _____

2. How many units are in the book? _____

3. How many lessons are in each unit? _____

4. Where is the grammar practice? _____

5. Look at the QR code [QR]. Find the icon on page 7. What does it mean? _____

   _____

6. Look at the ▢ I CAN STATEMENT . Find it on page 11. What does it tell you? _____

   _____

7. Look at this icon [Q]. Find it on page 13. What does it mean?

   _____

## 3 LEARN ABOUT YOUR APP

1. Look inside the front cover. Where can you go to download the Pearson Practice English app for StartUp? _____

2. Where are the instructions for registering for the app? _____

   _____

3. Look at the picture of the app. What do you see?

   _____

4. Look at the picture again. Fill in the blanks with the numbers 1–3.
   a. Number _____ shows the practice activities.
   b. Number _____ shows the video files.
   c. Number _____ shows the audio files.

5. Look at the picture again. What does this ☁ mean? _____

6. Look at the QR code on page 7 again. What happens when you scan the code? _____

   _____

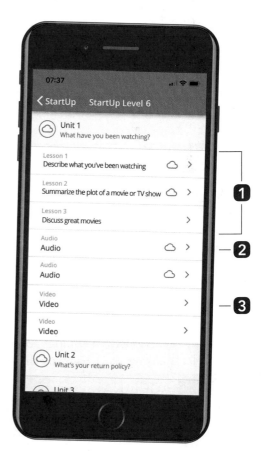

# TSW MEDIA
## MEET THE PEOPLE OF TSW MEDIA

*To find out more, watch the videos!*

**TSW Media** is a big company with big ideas. It has offices all over the world. It works with international clients to help them market their products and services.

### OSCAR BLANCO
Sound and video editor

▶00-02 I'm Oscar Blanco, and I'm a native of Bogota, Colombia. I'm a sound and video editor.

### GINA CARK
Human resources specialist

▶00-05 Hi, there. I'm Gina Cark, and I'm a human resources specialist from New York City.

### HANA LEE
Marketing and sales rep

▶00-03 Annyeonghaseyo! I'm Hana Lee, and I'm a marketing and sales rep from Seoul, South Korea.

### MICHAEL STEWART
Project manager

▶00-06 Hey, everybody. I'm Michael Stewart, and I'm a project manager in the Toronto office.

### PABLO PIÑEDA
Digital artist, animator, and illustrator

▶00-04 Hi! I'm Pablo Piñeda. I was born in Costa Rica, but I moved to New York City in my teens. Now, I'm a digital artist, animator, and illustrator.

### ELENA RUBIO
Market research specialist

▶00-07 Hello, I'm Elena Rubio. I live in Lima, Peru. I'm a market research specialist for Latin America.

Every year, TSW sponsors a competition for employees to get mentoring and coaching to improve their public speaking skills. Here are three of the winners!

### ADRIANA LOPEZ

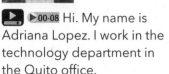

▶00-08 Hi. My name is Adriana Lopez. I work in the technology department in the Quito office.

### KENDRICK SCOTT

▶00-09 Hey! I'm Kendrick Scott and I'm a designer in the Vancouver office.

### DAVID CRUZ

▶00-10 Hi. My name is David Cruz. I'm from Florida, but I've lived and worked in Singapore for the past six years. I'm an advertising manager.

# WHAT HAVE YOU BEEN WATCHING?

## LEARNING GOALS

In this unit, you

⊘ describe what you've been watching

⊘ summarize the plot of a movie or TV show

⊘ discuss great movies

⊘ read about changes caused by technology

⊘ write about a movie or TV show

## GET STARTED

**A** Read the unit title and learning goals.

**B** Look at the photo. What's going on?

**C** Now read Oscar's message. How does he feel? Why?

OSCAR BLANCO
@OscarB

Arrived at the hotel last night. Stayed up late watching TV. So tired for my meeting this morning.

# LESSON 1 — DESCRIBE WHAT YOU'VE BEEN WATCHING

**OSCAR BLANCO**
@OscarB

I can't stop thinking about my new favorite TV show. How am I going to focus today?

## 1 VOCABULARY
Ways to describe movies or TV shows

**A** Look at the graph. What's the most popular movie genre? What's the least popular? Are you surprised? Why or why not?

**B** ▶01-01 Listen. Then listen and repeat.

> **dull:** not interesting or exciting
> **heartbreaking:** making you sad
> **heartwarming:** making you happy
> **hilarious:** extremely funny
> **imaginative:** containing new ideas
> **predictable:** happening how you expect
> **romantic:** showing feelings of love
> **scary:** making you afraid
> **silly:** stupid or not sensible
> **suspenseful:** making you nervous about the future
> **violent:** showing actions that hurt or kill people
> **weird:** unusual and strange

### MOST POPULAR MOVIE GENRES

- ACTION / ADVENTURE 40%
- COMEDY 26%
- DRAMA 16%
- SUSPENSE / THRILLER 8%
- DOCUMENTARY 1%
- OTHER 9%

**C** Complete the chart with words from 1B.

| Always positive | Sometimes positive or negative | Always negative |
|---|---|---|
| heartwarming | | |

**D** PAIRS  Which movie genres in 1A do you like or dislike? Why? Use the words in 1B.

*I don't like action and adventure movies because they are always violent and predictable.*

## 2 GRAMMAR  Present perfect continuous: Review and expand

Use the present perfect continuous to describe actions that started in the past and are still continuing. We sometimes use the present perfect continuous with adverbs of time such as *lately* and *recently* to show that something started in the recent past.

| Statements | | | | | | |
|---|---|---|---|---|---|---|
| **Subject** | ***Have / has*** | ***(Not)*** | ***Been*** | **Present participle** | | ***Lately / recently*** |
| I | have | (not) | been | watching | old movies | lately. |
| She | has | | | | | recently. |

| Questions | | | | | | |
|---|---|---|---|---|---|---|
| | ***Have / has*** | **Subject** | ***Been*** | **Present participle** | | ***Lately / recently?*** |
| | Have | you | been | watching | anything good | lately? |
| What | has | he | | | | recently? |

>> FOR PRACTICE, GO TO PAGE 125

# 3 CONVERSATION SKILL

**A** ▶01-02 Read the conversation skill. Listen. Notice how Speaker B responds with different degrees of enthusiasm.

1. **Not enthusiastic** B: Hmm. I don't know.
2. **Enthusiastic** B: Oh, yeah? What did you see?
3. **Very enthusiastic** B: Wow! That's fantastic!

> **Express degrees of enthusiasm**
>
> To show a lot of enthusiasm, use words like *wow* and *great*. Words like *really* and phrases like *oh, yeah* show some enthusiasm, and words like *oh* and *hmm* show less enthusiasm. You can also add more stress and a sharper rise-fall intonation to show more enthusiasm. A flat voice shows a lack of enthusiasm.

**B** ▶01-03 Listen. How enthusiastic is Speaker B? Check (✓) the correct box.

|   | Not enthusiastic | Enthusiastic | Very enthusiastic |
|---|---|---|---|
| 1 |   |   |   |
| 2 |   |   |   |
| 3 |   |   |   |

# 4 CONVERSATION

**A** ▶01-04 Listen or watch. What do Oscar and Hana talk about?

**B** ▶01-05 Listen or watch again. Complete the chart about Oscar's new favorite show.

| Title | Genre | Ways Oscar describes it | Ways Hana describes it |
|---|---|---|---|
|   |   |   |   |

**C** ▶01-06 FOCUS ON LANGUAGE Listen or watch. Complete the conversation.

> Do you think Hana will watch *Doctor Who*? Why or why not?

Oscar: Have you _____ anything good lately?

Hana: I have. I've been watching some really great old movies.

Oscar: _____ ? Like what?

Hana: You know, the old blockbusters like *Citizen Kane*, *Gone with the Wind*, and *Casablanca*. Last night I saw *Titanic*. What a(n) _____ story!

# 5 TRY IT YOURSELF

**A** THINK Choose a TV series you've been watching. Take notes about the title, genre, and ways to describe it.

**B** PAIRS Student A: Tell your partner about what you've been watching. Use your notes from 5A. Student B: Ask questions and respond with degrees of enthusiasm. Use the conversation in 4C as an example.

**C** REPORT Tell the class about what your partner has been watching. Have any students been watching the same series?

■ I CAN **DESCRIBE WHAT I'VE BEEN WATCHING.**

**OSCAR BLANCO**
@OscarB

Anybody know why the movie
*Titanic* was so popular? Am I the
only person in the world who has
never seen it?

## 1 VOCABULARY
Elements of a movie or TV show

**A** Look at the photo and read the caption.
What information is new to you?

 The movie *Titanic* cost **$200 million** to make. Filming the movie
was **more expensive than building the original ship**, which
cost **$7.5 million** in **1912**. The movie **earned** **$2.18 billion**,
making it one of the **most successful** movies in history.

**B** ▶01-07 Listen. Then listen and repeat.

**a narrator:** the person who tells a story

**a plot:** the story that is told in a book,
movie, TV show, or play

**a setting:** the place and time a story
happens

**a role:** a character in a story

**a scene:** a short part of a movie, TV show,
or play

**dialog:** the conversation between
characters in a story

**a soundtrack:** the music that is played
during a movie or TV show

**a special effect:** an unusual image or sound
that occurs in a movie or TV show

**cinematography:** the skill or art of movie
photography

**C** ▶01-08 Listen. Which movie element is each speaker describing? Use words from 1B.

1. _____    3. _____    5. _____

2. _____    4. _____    6. _____

**D** PAIRS Name a movie or TV show for each category. Say why you chose it.

| **Best Soundtrack** | **Most Beautiful Cinematography** | **Scariest Setting** |
|---|---|---|
| _____ | _____ | _____ |
| **Most Imaginative Plot** | **Most Romantic Dialog** | **Most Interesting Special Effects** |
| _____ | _____ | _____ |

## 2 GRAMMAR *What* clauses for emphasis

Start sentences with *what* clauses to emphasize the topic or main point.

| *What* clause | *Be* | Topic or main point |
|---|---|---|
| What I like best | is | the dialog. |
| What amazes me | | |
| What she didn't love | was | |
| What impressed them | | |

**Note:** The noun or pronoun in the *what* clause can be the subject or object:
**Subject:** *What **Mary** likes best is the acting.* **Object:** *What amazed **Mary** was the acting.*

>> FOR PRACTICE, GO TO PAGE 126

# 3 PRONUNCIATION

**A** ▶01-09 Read and listen to the pronunciation note.

> **What clauses**
>
> There is usually a pause after a *what* clause that begins a sentence. The topic following the *what* clause usually has the main stress. *What I liked best/ was the plot.*

**B** ▶01-10 Listen. Notice the pause and main stress in each sentence. Then listen and repeat.

1. What I like best/ is the **soundtrack**.
2. What amazed me/ was the **dialog**.
3. What confused me/ was the **plot**.
4. What impressed me/ was the narrator's **voice**.

**C** ▶01-11 Listen. Place a slash (/) where you hear a pause. Place a large dot over the topic.

1. What I liked best was the food.
2. What impressed Marco was the band.
3. What surprised Nora was the setting.
4. What she didn't like was the music.

**D** PAIRS Practice the sentences in 3C. Then describe what you liked most or least about a festival, movie, or concert you saw recently.

*What I liked most about the movie/ was the acting.*

# 4 CONVERSATION

**A** ▶01-12 Listen or watch. What do Hana and Oscar talk about?

**B** ▶01-13 Listen or watch again. Answer the questions.

1. What movie has Oscar never seen before?
2. What does Hana like best about the movie?
3. Why does Hana like the movie's two stars?
4. How do Oscar and Hana summarize the movie?

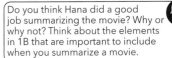

**C** ▶01-14 FOCUS ON LANGUAGE Listen or watch. Complete the conversation.

> Do you think Hana did a good job summarizing the movie? Why or why not? Think about the elements in 1B that are important to include when you summarize a movie.

Hana: The _____ of the movie is the *Titanic* in the year 1912, so that part is real. But it's not a documentary—it's a love story.

Oscar: Oh.

Hana: _____ is the main character, Rose. She's played by two different actresses.

Oscar: Really?

Hana: Yep. We first see Rose as an old woman in 1996. She's the _____ of the story and one of the last living survivors of the *Titanic*.

# 5 TRY IT YOURSELF

**A** THINK What movie or TV show do you think other people should watch? Why? Take notes about each of the elements of the movie or TV show in the box.

| title | stars | setting | plot | soundtrack | favorite scene | what I like best about it |
| --- | --- | --- | --- | --- | --- | --- |

**B** PAIRS Student A: Summarize the movie or TV show from 5A. Student B: Ask questions to get more information. Use the conversation in 4C as an example.

**C** TAKE A POLL List the movies and TV shows from 5A. Which are the most popular in the class? Least popular?

■ I CAN SUMMARIZE THE PLOT OF A MOVIE OR TV SHOW.

## OSCAR BLANCO
@OscarB

The first feature-length film was made in 1906. Can you guess how many movies have been made since then?

## 1 BEFORE YOU LISTEN

**A** When was the last time you saw a great movie? What did you like about it?

**B** ▶01-15 VOCABULARY  Listen. Then listen and repeat.

> **a classic:** considered important or high quality, with a value that lasts for a long time
> **an emotion:** a strong feeling, such as love, hate, or sadness
> **an achievement:** something difficult that is done successfully
> **touch:** to affect someone's emotions, especially for sympathy or sadness
> **innovative:** using or inventing good new ideas and methods
> **a vision:** an idea of what you think something should be like
> **inspire:** to make someone have a particular feeling or act in a certain way
> **engage:** to make someone stay interested in something

**C** Complete the sentences with words from 1B.

1. The movie didn't _____ me at all. I was bored the whole time.
2. The goal of our nature documentary is to _____ people to love and protect endangered animals.
3. The director used a(n) _____ camera technique to film the movie. It had never been tried before.
4. Filming a movie on Mars would be a big _____ .
5. I tried not to show any _____ , but I was crying by the end of the movie.
6. Movies about people helping other people _____ us deeply and make us all feel more connected.
7. It was a good movie, but I don't think it's a(n) _____ . Ten years from now, nobody will remember it.
8. The actor didn't agree with the director's _____ for his character.

## 2 GRAMMAR  *By* to explain how

Use *by* with gerunds to explain how something is done.

| Main clause | *By* | Gerund | |
|---|---|---|---|
| The director created the sounds | by | recording | angry elephants. |
| ***By*** | **Gerund** | | **Main clause** |
| By | experimenting | with new techniques, | this team pushed technology to new limits. |

Notes
* Do not use a comma before the *by* phrase when it comes after the main clause.
* Use a comma after the *by* phrase when it comes before the main clause.

**>> FOR PRACTICE, GO TO PAGE 127**

## 3 LISTENING

**A** ▶01-16 Listen or watch. What is the main idea of the talk?

**B** ▶01-17 Read the Listening Skill. Listen or watch again. Complete the examples for each idea.

| Great movies affect our emotions. |
| --- |
| 1. They don't just move us to tears–they also _____ out loud, and even cause us to jump out of our seats in _____ . |
| 2. We _____ Rick's pain as he says good-bye. |

| Great movies are innovative. |
| --- |
| 3. To film the epic space battles, they built a fleet of miniature _____ . |
| 4. They created the sound of spaceships screeching across the universe by recording _____ driving on a wet highway and combining these sounds with the sounds of angry _____ . |

Adriana Lopez I TSW Global Speaker Program
**Unit 1: What Makes a Movie a Classic?**

**LISTENING SKILL**
**Listen for examples**

Listen for examples to help you visualize (picture in your mind) a speaker's ideas.

**C** ▶01-18 Listen or watch again. Answer the questions.

1. What difficult decision does Rick have to make in *Casablanca*?
   _____

2. What does the audience learn about from watching *Casablanca*?
   _____

3. What did George Lucas need to do before he could make *Star Wars*? Why?
   _____

4. How did the first audiences respond to *Star Wars*?
   _____

**D** VOCABULARY EXPANSION Read each sentence from the talk. What do the underlined expressions mean?

1. Movies have the power to touch us. They don't just <u>move us to tears</u>–they also make us laugh out loud, and even cause us to jump out of our seats in fear.
   _____

2. Working night and day in a warehouse, this talented group of young artists and engineers <u>let their imaginations run wild</u>.
   _____

3. Some great movies touch our emotions deeply, and some <u>break new ground</u> technologically.
   _____

**E** PAIRS Compare answers in 3D.

Watch the final scene of *Casablanca*. Did it touch your emotions?

## 4 DISCUSSION

**A** THINK Do you agree with the speaker's opinions? What are some other things that make a movie great? Give examples.

**B** DISCUSS In small groups, share your opinions and examples from 4A.

**C** EVALUATE Write your opinions from 4B on the board. As a class, vote on the five most important things that make a movie great.

☐ I CAN DISCUSS GREAT MOVIES.

**OSCAR BLANCO**
@OscarB

Just read this interview about how much film technology has changed. I wonder what movies will be like five or ten years from now?

## 1 BEFORE YOU READ

**A**   PAIRS   Has technology changed films during your lifetime? How?

**B**   ▶01-19 VOCABULARY   Listen. Then listen and repeat. Do you know these words?

| a transition    adapt    disastrous    an extra    virtual reality    an impact |
| --- |

**>> FOR DEFINITIONS AND PRACTICE, GO TO PAGE 127**

## 2 READ

**A**   PREVIEW   Read the title and look at the photos. What do you think the interview will be about?

**B**   ▶01-20 Read and listen to the interview. Was your prediction correct?

## Technology Changed Everything About How We Watch Movies

Film historian Lois Clark has written a new book about the history of film technology. She agreed to talk with us about how technology has changed the film industry and the lives of the people who work in it.

Raymond Griffith, a star from the Silent Era

**Interviewer: What do you consider the most important change in the 20th century?**

Lois Clark: Without a doubt, the introduction of full-length "talkies" in 1927. Before then, audiences would watch silent films. In these films, they could see the actors' lips moving, but they couldn't hear any words. Dialog cards
5  appeared on the screen after the lines were spoken.

**I: So theaters were totally silent back then?**

LC: Actually, most theaters hired musicians who sat below the screen and played music that matched the mood of each scene—fast, loud music during the action and slow, soft music for romantic scenes. The film *The*
10 *Jazz Singer* changed all that. It featured the first words ever spoken in a film, "Wait a minute. Wait a minute. You ain't heard nothing yet!" Audiences were astonished.

**I: Wow. That must have really been a game changer.**

LC: Totally. Only two years later, almost all Hollywood films were talkies. Not
15 only did this change the way we watch movies, but it also had a major impact on the industry. Some stars like Joan Crawford and Laurel and Hardy made successful transitions from the Silent Era to the talkies. But for others, the introduction of sound was disastrous. Some of these actors couldn't adapt well to expressing themselves with words instead of facial expressions and
20 motions. Others struggled because of their voices. Raymond Griffith had been a famous actor during the Silent Era. However, he had lost his voice when he was young and could only speak quietly. When the talkies took over, Griffith's career as an actor came to an end, and he is almost completely forgotten today.

25 **I: Aside from the introduction of sound, what else most changed movies?**

LC: The biggest visual innovation has been the development of CGI, computer-generated imagery.

**I: How so?**

LC: Before, what audiences saw was in some way real. For example, films
30 advertised as having a cast of thousands really had thousands of extras. The 1982 movie *Gandhi* holds the record for using more than 300,000 extras in the funeral scene shot in Delhi. Today, it would be inconceivable to use so many people. Even in 2000, *Gladiator* was using CGI instead of extras. The crowd in the fight scenes included more than 30,000 CGI spectators instead of
35 real people.

**>>**

3-D movies have never really caught on.

> **I: What changes can we expect in the future?**
> **LC:** Who knows? One hundred years ago, few people could imagine hearing actors' voices in a film. Since then, there have been a lot of successes and failures. Drones have completely changed the way aerial shots are filmed. 3-D
40 movies, on the other hand, have never really become as popular as expected, despite the early success of *Avatar*. They are just too expensive for film studios to make, and many viewers don't enjoy wearing 3-D glasses. Nowadays, everyone is wondering if virtual reality can be the next big thing. I'm sure in the future, there will be ways to experience films that we can't even imagine right
45 now. All I know is that it's exciting to think about what the next breakthrough will be and how it could change movies forever.

## 3 CHECK YOUR UNDERSTANDING

**A** Read the interview again. What is the main idea?

**B** Answer the questions, according to the interview.

1.  How did audiences know what the actors were saying when the movies were silent?
    _____

2.  What happened to the actors from the Silent Era after most Hollywood films became talkies?
    _____

3.  How did the introduction of CGI change movies?
    _____

4.  How do you think Lois Clark feels about technological changes in the future?
    _____

**C** CLOSE READING Reread lines 7–10 in the interview. Then circle the correct answer.

In line 10, what does the word *that* refer to?
  a.  musicians playing live music in movie theaters
  b.  the moods of the films
  c.  where the musicians sat in the theaters

| READING SKILL **Recognize jargon** |
| --- |
| Jargon refers to the words and phrases that are used mainly by people who belong to the same professional group and that are difficult for others to understand. |

**D** Read the Reading Skill. Use your own words to explain the meaning of the jargon used in the interview. Complete the chart.

| Jargon | Meaning in your own words |
| --- | --- |
| 1. talkies | |
| 2. a game changer | |
| 3. the Silent Era | |
| 4. a cast of thousands | |

**E** PAIRS What is the interview about? Retell the most important ideas. Use your own words.

## 4 MAKE IT PERSONAL

Research today's top three movies. How much does each depend on CGI? 🔍

**A** THINK How has technology changed the industry you work in now or want to work in? What changes would you like to see in the future? Take notes.

**B** PAIRS Share your ideas.

☐ I CAN READ ABOUT CHANGES CAUSED BY TECHNOLOGY.

# LESSON 5 — WRITE ABOUT A MOVIE OR TV SHOW

**OSCAR BLANCO**
@OscarB

I used to work on TV shows. Now I watch…a lot of them! I want to tell you about my favorite show of all time.

## 1 BEFORE YOU WRITE

**A** What kinds of movies or TV shows do you enjoy watching the most?

**B** Complete the sentences with the words in the box.

> believable    compelling

1. This show takes place in a neighborhood just like mine. It's really _____.
2. The movie was so _____ that I forgot to eat my popcorn.

**C** Read Oscar's blog. What TV show does Oscar describe? Does he make you want to watch it?

---

Blog | About | Contact                                    🔍 Search

### Reasons to Love *The Big Bang Theory*!

For a long time, my favorite TV show has been *The Big Bang Theory*. It's a comedy program about a group of friends who live and work in California. The characters are all super-smart scientists except for one, Penny, who's a waitress and an actress. Amazingly, she's the one who usually makes the best decisions. Most of the characters live in apartments in the same building. The setting of the show is usually in one of these apartments, but sometimes we also see the characters in other places, such as in their university offices.

The main reason I love this show is the imaginative characters. Some of them are married, some are single, and there's a mix of men and women. What I like about them is that even though they have completely different personalities, they're all equals. There isn't one main character. Most of all, I like that they seem very believable, with real joys and problems. Plus, they're all hilarious!

Another reason this show is my favorite is the compelling story. Although the characters, their jobs, and their homes have stayed the same, each episode is totally different. One might be about Penny's acting career, the next might be about a visit from a character's annoying mother, and another might be about all the funny problems with planning a wedding. Whatever the plot of an episode is, I know it will entertain me and make me laugh.

If you're not already a huge fan of *The Big Bang Theory*, I'm sure you'll enjoy watching it. With its interesting characters and story, it will definitely become one of your favorite shows.

*About*
*RSS Feed*
*Social Media*
*Recent Posts*
*Archives*
*Email*

**Leave a Reply**

Enter your comment here…

---

**D** Read the blog again. Take notes in the chart.

> **Main idea of blog**
> _____
> _____

> **Supporting reason 1**
> _____
> _____

> **Supporting reason 2**
> _____
> _____

> **Conclusion**
> _____
> _____

# 2 FOCUS ON WRITING

**A** Read the Writing Skill. Then reread Oscar's blog. Underline the topic sentence in each paragraph.

**B** Analyze each topic sentence.
1. Circle the transition words.
2. Put a box around the main ideas.
3. Check (✓) the controlling ideas.
4. Are these strong topic sentences? Why or why not?

---

**WRITING SKILL** Write a strong topic sentence

Topic sentences help readers understand the main idea of a paragraph. A *strong* topic sentence usually refers back to the main idea of the entire text. It also:
- uses transition words to make connections between paragraphs.
- includes the main idea of the paragraph.
- has a controlling idea, which is the idea you want to explain in more detail in the paragraph.

For example:

transition words     main idea           controlling idea

*The first reason I like the movie is because the acting is great.*

---

# 3 PLAN YOUR WRITING

**A** THINK What is your favorite movie or TV show? What do you like about it? Draw a chart like the one in 1D.

**B** PAIRS Explain why this movie or TV show is your favorite.

*My favorite movie of all time is Love Actually. I've probably watched it more than twenty times already. One of the things that I love about this movie is...*

**Pre-writing tip**
Try replaying what you've seen and heard in your mind. This will help you remember what happened.

# 4 WRITE

Write a blog about your favorite movie or TV show. Be sure to include two or three reasons why it is your favorite. Remember to use a strong topic sentence for each main paragraph. Use the blog in 1C as a model.

# 5 REVISE YOUR WRITING

**A** PAIRS Exchange blogs and read each other's writing.
1. Did your partner use a strong topic sentence for each main paragraph? Underline each topic sentence.
2. Did your partner include two or three reasons why it was his or her favorite movie or TV show? List them.

**B** PAIRS Can your partner improve his or her blog? Make suggestions.

# 6 PROOFREAD

Read your blog again. Check your
- spelling
- punctuation
- capitalization

# PUT IT TOGETHER

## 1 PRESENTATION PROJECT

▶️ **A** ▶01-21 Listen or watch. What is the presentation about?

▶️ **B** ▶01-22 Listen or watch again. Answer the questions.

1. What kind of movies and TV shows does Junio like best?

   _____

2. What three reasons does Junio give?

   _____

**C** Read the presentation skill. Why do you think this skill is important?

**D** Make your own presentation.

> **PRESENTATION SKILL**
>
> **Stay calm**
> Before you begin speaking, relax by pausing, making eye contact with your audience, and taking a deep breath.

**Step 1** Lesson 1 is about kinds of movies and TV shows. Think about your favorite kind of movie or TV show. Why do you prefer this kind?

**Step 2** Prepare a two-minute presentation about your favorite kind of movie or TV show. Include several reasons why you like it. Bring an item or picture that is related to your presentation.

**Step 3** Give your presentation to the class. Remember to use the presentation skill. Answer questions and get feedback.

> How did you do? Complete the self-evaluation on page 165.

## 2 REFLECT AND PLAN

**A** Look back through the unit. Check (✓) the things you learned. Highlight the things you need to learn.

**Speaking objectives**
- ☐ Describe what you've been watching
- ☐ Summarize the plot of a movie or TV show
- ☐ Discuss great movies

**Vocabulary**
- ☐ Ways to describe movies or TV shows
- ☐ Elements of a movie or TV show

**Conversation**
- ☐ Express degrees of enthusiasm

**Pronunciation**
- ☐ *What* clauses

**Listening**
- ☐ Listen for examples

**Grammar**
- ☐ Present perfect continuous
- ☐ *What* clauses for emphasis
- ☐ *By* to explain how

**Reading**
- ☐ Recognize jargon

**Writing**
- ☐ Write a strong topic sentence

**B** What will you do to learn the things you highlighted? For example, use your app, review your Student Book, or do other practice. Make a plan.

> ‹ Notes          Done
>
> In the app, do the Lesson 2 Vocabulary activities: Elements of a movie or TV show.
>
> _____
> _____
> _____
> _____

# 2 WHAT'S YOUR RETURN POLICY?

## LEARNING GOALS

In this unit, you
- ⊘ ask about a return policy
- ⊘ discuss taking out a loan
- ⊘ talk about crowdfunding
- ⊘ read about the health benefits of giving
- ⊘ write an email to dispute a problem

## GET STARTED

**A** Read the unit title and learning goals.

**B** Look at the photo. What's going on?

**C** Now read Pablo's message. How does he feel about shopping?

PABLO PIÑEDA
@PabloP

People who say money can't buy happiness just don't know where to go shopping.

**PABLO PIÑEDA**
@PabloP

My friend just took some amazing pictures with his drone. Now I want one for myself.

## 1 VOCABULARY  Return policy language

**A** Look at the reasons why people return things. Which do you think is the most common? Why? What other reasons do people have for returning things?

**Five Reasons for Returning Products**

| It's defective. | It's damaged. | It's the wrong size. | It's the wrong color. | I don't want it anymore. |

**B** ▶02-01 Listen. Then listen and repeat.

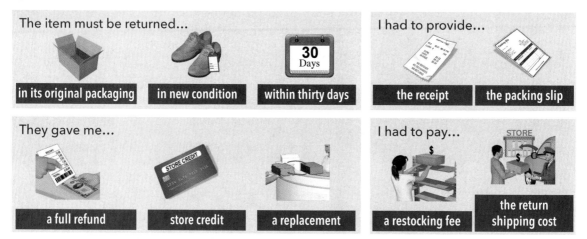

The item must be returned...

| in its original packaging | in new condition | within thirty days |

I had to provide...

| the receipt | the packing slip |

They gave me...

| a full refund | store credit | a replacement |

I had to pay...

| a restocking fee | the return shipping cost |

**C** PAIRS  Talk about a time when you returned something. What did you have to do? Did you get your money back? Did you have to pay any extra costs or fees? Use the words in 1B.

## 2 GRAMMAR  *As long as, providing (that), unless*

We can use the conjunctions *as long as*, *providing (that)*, and *unless* in conditional clauses.

| Result clause | | | Conditional clause | | | |
|---|---|---|---|---|---|---|
| Subject | Future verb or Modal + verb | | Conjunction | | Simple present | |
| You | can return | it | providing (that) | you | have | the packing slip. |
| We | will give | you a refund | as long as | | | |
| They | can't return | it | unless | they | | |

**Notes**
- Use *unless* to mean *if…not* or *except…if*. Use it about something that could happen if something else does not happen.
- Use *as long as* and *providing (that)* to show that something will only be possible if something else happens or is done first.

>> FOR PRACTICE, GO TO PAGE 128

# 3 CONVERSATION SKILL

**A** ▶02-02 Read the conversation skill. Listen. Notice that Speaker A makes a statement and Speaker B asks a question for clarification.

1. **A:** You have to return the shirt within thirty days to get a full refund.

   **B:** Do you mean that I won't get all my money back after thirty days?

2. **A:** You're responsible for the return shipping cost if you return the item.

   **B:** So I'll have to pay to send it back to you?

**B** PAIRS Practice the conversations.

# 4 CONVERSATION

**A** ▶02-03 Listen or watch. What is the conversation about?

**B** ▶02-04 Listen or watch again. Then answer the questions.

1. What is Pablo trying to buy?
2. Why is the AirEye 2100 a good choice?
3. Why can't Pablo buy it at the store?

 Does the store's return policy seem fair? Why or why not?

**C** ▶02-05 FOCUS ON LANGUAGE Listen or watch. Complete the conversation.

| | |
|---|---|
| Pablo: | What's your return policy if I buy something online? |
| Store assistant: | Well, you can either return it here or to one of our other stores, or you can ship it back. Just remember to keep your _____ . |
| Pablo: | And I can get a full refund? |
| Store assistant: | That's correct. _____ you return it within thirty days and it's in its original packaging, you can get your money back. |
| Pablo: | _____ you're saying that if I want to return it, I need to return the box as well? |
| Store assistant: | Right. |

# 5 TRY IT YOURSELF

**A** THINK Imagine you own a store. Create a return policy for the store. Complete the chart.

| | |
|---|---|
| What can customers buy at your store? | |
| What rules do customers have to follow to return an item? | |
| Do customers have to pay any extra fees? | |

**B** ROLE PLAY Student A: Ask about the return policy for Student B's store. Ask questions for clarification. Use the conversation in 4C as an example.

**C** COMPARE Share your return policies with the class. Are some fairer than others? Why?

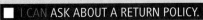 ■ I CAN ASK ABOUT A RETURN POLICY.

PABLO PIÑEDA
@PabloP

Looking forward to getting my first car! So much research to do!

 **1 VOCABULARY** Language for loans

**A** Look at the infographic. Do any of the reasons for taking out a loan surprise you? Why?

| **Why do people take out loans?** | | | | | | | |
|---|---|---|---|---|---|---|---|
| to pay off bills | to pay for school | to buy a home | to buy a car | to fix a home | to take a vacation | to pay for a wedding | to start a business |

**B** ▶02-06 Listen. Then listen and repeat.

**Loan verbs**

**take out:** to get something in an official way, such as a loan

**shop around:** to check a lot of places for the best price or deal

**qualify:** to have the right to have or do something

**be turned down:** to not be accepted for something

**pay off:** to give back the money that you owe for something

**be approved:** to get official permission to do something

**Loan nouns**

**an interest rate:** the extra amount that a bank charges when you borrow money

**a credit score:** a number that shows how likely you are to pay back borrowed money

**a credit history:** a record of how often you have borrowed money and paid it back

**a down payment:** the first, usually large, amount of money you pay for something, with the rest to be paid later

**C** ▶02-07 Listen. What loan language is being talked about? Write words from 1B.

1. _____    3. _____    5. _____
2. _____    4. _____    6. _____

## 2 GRAMMAR  Past unreal conditional

Use the past unreal conditional to talk about untrue or imagined situations and their results in the past. We can use it to say how someone could have gotten better results.

| Result clause | | | If-clause | | | |
|---|---|---|---|---|---|---|
| | Modal | *Have* + past participle | *If* | *If* | Past perfect | |
| You | might could would | have gotten | a better interest rate | if you | had gone | to a different bank. |

**Note:** Use *might* or *could* in the result clause when you are uncertain of the result. Use *would* in the result clause when you are certain.

**>> FOR PRACTICE, GO TO PAGE 129**

# 3 PRONUNCIATION

**A** ▶02-08 Read and listen to the pronunciation note.

**B** ▶02-09 Listen. Notice the reduction of *have* to /əv/ and the blending and stress in past modals. Then listen and repeat.

1. I would have gȯtten a loan if my credit score had been better.
2. Pablo might have boȯught that car if the price had been lower.
3. Lisa cȯuldn't have tȧken out a loan.

**C** ▶02-10 Listen and complete the sentences. Then listen again and repeat.

1. I _____ the down payment without my parents' help.
2. Pablo _____ to take the bus if he hadn't bought a car.
3. The bank _____ the loan if you hadn't had a full-time job.
4. If Nora had qualified for a loan, she _____ her own business.

**Blend past modals**

The auxiliary *have* is reduced to /əv/ and is linked to the preceding past modal like *could*, *would*, and *might*. When the past modal is affirmative, stress the past participle and reduce *have* to /əv/. When the past modal is negative, stress the past participle and the modal and reduce *have* to /əv/.

# 4 CONVERSATION

**A** ▶02-11 Listen or watch. What is Pablo having trouble with?

**B** ▶02-12 Listen or watch again. Answer the questions.

1. Why does Pablo want to buy a used car?
2. What advice does Gina give Pablo?
3. What does Pablo plan to do this weekend?

**C** ▶02-13 FOCUS ON LANGUAGE Listen or watch. Complete the conversation.

Do you think Pablo will get a better deal on his car loan? Why or why not?

| | |
|---|---|
| Pablo: | I'm having a little trouble getting a loan. |
| Gina: | Oh, that's too bad. |
| Pablo: | It turns out I have a great credit score, but I don't have much _____ . I've only had a credit card for a few years, and I've never needed to borrow a lot of money before. |
| Gina: | So they _____ for the loan? |
| Pablo: | Well, no. But the guy at the car dealership said that if my overall credit had been better, I _____ qualified for a lower interest rate. |

# 5 TRY IT YOURSELF

**A** THINK Which of these loans would be the best for Pablo? Why?

| Loan 1 | Loan 2 | Loan 3 |
|---|---|---|
| Down payment: $1,000 | Down payment: $3,000 | Down payment: $2,000 |
| Interest rate: 6 percent | Interest rate: 4 percent | Interest rate: 8 percent |
| Length of loan: 5 years | Length of loan: 4 years | Length of loan: 3 years |

**B** PAIRS Discuss your ideas. Do you have the same opinion?

**C** TAKE A POLL What do most people think? Why?      ☐ I CAN DISCUSS TAKING OUT A LOAN.

### PABLO PIÑEDA
@PabloP

Just watched a talk about crowdfunding. Did you know that even Mozart used it?

## 1 BEFORE YOU LISTEN

**A** What do you think of when you hear the word *crowdfunding*?

**B** ▶02-14 VOCABULARY Listen. Then listen and repeat.

> **finance:** to provide money, especially a large amount of money, to pay for something
> **raise:** to collect money to help people
> **viral:** spreading very quickly to many people, especially through the internet
> **a phenomenon:** something in society or nature that happens or exists
> **a donation:** money that you give to help a person or an organization
> **invest:** to give money in order to get a profit later
> **a scam:** a dishonest plan to get money by tricking people
> **a risk:** the chance that something bad may happen
> **a fundraising campaign:** an activity done to collect money for a charity, school, or something else

**C** Complete the sentences with words from 1B.

1. Every year I make a _____ to help poor children in my city.
2. Crowdfunding is not a new _____ .
3. For our _____ we sold candy to raise money for the football team.
4. Tom has a great idea for a product, and he's looking for someone to _____ it.
5. Many people _____ money in their home so that its value will increase.
6. Jim wants to borrow money from me, but I don't want to take the _____ . He might not pay me back.
7. Don't believe that ad you found online. It's a _____ .
8. My cousin's cat video went _____ last week. It got over 500,000 views!
9. She's trying to _____ money for her co-worker. He was hurt and can't work.

## 2 GRAMMAR Connectives to express contrast and surprise

> We use connectives such as *despite, however, although, even though, on the other hand*, and *while* to contrast two different aspects of the same person, thing, or situation. These words introduce an opposing idea, especially one that the listener or reader does not expect.
>
> He meant the campaign as a joke. **However**, the request went viral and he raised a lot of money.
>
> People feel like they're making a difference **even though** they're giving small amounts.
>
> **Despite** some risks to investors, the popularity of crowdfunding has exploded.
>
> Notes
> - Connectives like *however* and *on the other hand* are used to connect a sentence to the previous sentence. They are followed immediately by a comma.
> - *While, although*, and *even though* connect clauses within a sentence. When these words begin a sentence, add a comma between the clauses.
> - *Despite* and *in spite of* are followed by a noun phrase. When they begin a sentence, add a comma at the end of the noun phrase.

>> FOR PRACTICE, GO TO PAGE 130

# 3 LISTENING

▶️ **Ⓐ** ▶02-15 Listen or watch. What is the main idea of the talk?

▶️ **Ⓑ** ▶02-16 Read the Listening Skill. Listen or watch again. How does the introduction catch the listeners' interest? How does the conclusion connect the topic to the listener?

▶️ **Ⓒ** ▶02-17 Listen or watch again. Answer the questions.

1. What was the most famous bizarre crowdfunding campaign?
   _____
   _____

2. How did Mozart use crowdfunding?
   _____
   _____

3. What kinds of campaigns is crowdfunding used for now?
   _____
   _____

4. Why do creators like crowdfunding?
   _____
   _____

5. Why do investors like crowdfunding?
   _____
   _____

> **LISTENING SKILL**
> **Listen for the introduction and conclusion**
>
> In most talks, a speaker begins with an introduction and ends with a conclusion to help focus the listener on the topic or main idea.
>
> The introduction may ask also questions or tell stories to catch the listeners' interest.
>
> The conclusion may connect the topic to the listener or invite the listener to think about the future.

**Ⓓ** VOCABULARY EXPANSION  Read each sentence from the talk. What do the underlined expressions mean?

1. Since 2010, crowdfunding has become <u>mainstream</u>, bringing in billions of dollars every year.
   _____

2. But despite some risk to investors, the popularity of crowdfunding has <u>exploded</u>.
   _____

3. And, in terms of products, people love being <u>in on the ground floor</u> of exciting new business ideas.
   _____

**Ⓔ** PAIRS  Compare answers in 3D.

# 4 DISCUSSION

**Ⓐ** THINK  Have you ever taken part in crowdfunding? If so, what was your experience? If not, would you want to try it? Why or why not?

**Ⓑ** DISCUSS  In pairs, share your experiences and opinions from 4A.

**Ⓒ** REPORT  Tell the class about your partner's experiences and opinions.

I CAN **TALK ABOUT CROWDFUNDING.**

_(Video still: Kendrick Scott / TSW Global Speaker Program — Unit 2: Crowdfunding: Here to Stay?)_

**PABLO PIÑEDA**
@PabloP

Did you know that giving can make you healthier? I didn't.

## 1 BEFORE YOU READ

**A**   PAIRS   How often do you help other people? What kinds of things do you do?

**B**   ▶02-18 VOCABULARY   Listen. Then listen and repeat. Do you know these words?

| | | | |
|---|---|---|---|
| a shelter | a mood | make a difference | generous |
| blood pressure | a perspective | | |

**>> FOR DEFINITIONS AND PRACTICE, GO TO PAGE 130**

## 2 READ

**A**   PREVIEW   Read the title and the subheadings. Look at the photos. What do you think the article will be about?

**B**   ▶02-19 Read and listen to the article. Was your prediction correct?

# GIVING REALLY IS GOOD FOR YOU

For weeks after Leslie lost the job she loved, she felt terrible. Then, one day after another disappointing job interview, she passed a homeless shelter and decided on the spot
5 to volunteer there. Just making the decision made her feel good, and since then, her mood has improved a lot.

"I started volunteering because I wanted to make a difference in people's lives," she said,
10 "but since I've started working here, I feel much better. I think volunteering is helping me more than it's helping them."

Leslie's situation isn't really that unusual. People often feel good when they give their time,
15 money, or things to a good cause. What is more surprising, though, is that there is a lot of scientific research that proves giving really is good for our mental and physical health.

### Better Mental Health

20 When researchers at the University of Oregon studied the brains of nineteen women, they discovered something interesting. The pleasure areas in the women's brains lit up, or became more active, when these women
25 chose to donate some money to charity. When we give, our brain chemistry actually changes. Our brains release chemicals, such as serotonin and oxycodone, that make us feel happier.

Giving doesn't just make us
30 happier. It also reduces our stress. Researchers at Yale University and UCLA (University of California, Los Angeles) figured this out by studying the lives of seventy-
35 seven adults. They asked the adults to keep track of two things: how many times each day they felt stressed out and how often they did kind things for others. The people who were kind to others more often were less affected by stress.

### Better Physical Health

40 Being generous doesn't just affect how we feel. Researchers at the University of California and the University of British Columbia have learned that it can also lower people's blood pressure. The researchers gave
45 some money to seventy-three adults with high blood pressure. They told half the adults to spend the money on themselves and the other half to spend the money on other people. After six weeks, the people who had spent the money on other people had lower blood pressure
50 than the people who had spent the money on themselves. Being generous can not only lower our blood pressure, but it can also help us live longer. Researchers at the University of Michigan determined this by studying 423 elderly couples for five years. They discovered that the elderly
55 people who helped others were more than 50 percent more likely to live longer than those who didn't.

>>

> Giving Can Take Many Forms

Overall, the research showed that it doesn't really matter how or what you give. Whether you donate millions of
60 dollars to medical research or spend an hour a week talking to a lonely person, you can get the same health benefits.

Now, Leslie is still looking for a new job, but volunteering has given her a whole new perspective on life.
65 "The experience has taught me so much," she said. "I'm starting to realize that it really is better to give than receive."

## 3 CHECK YOUR UNDERSTANDING

**A** Read the article again. What is the main idea?

**B** Answer the questions, according to the article.

1. How did Leslie's mood change after she started volunteering?

_____

2. What happens to people's brain chemistry when they give?

_____

3. How does giving affect people's blood pressure?

_____

4. Does it matter how or what we give? Why or why not?

_____

**C** CLOSE READING  Reread lines 58–62 in the article. Then circle the correct answer.

How is the second sentence connected to the first sentence?
a. It provides a counterargument.
b. It give examples to support an argument.
c. It asks readers to give their opinion about an argument.

**D** Read the Reading Skill. Then reread the article and complete the chart.

| The information | The source of the information | READING SKILL<br>Identify sources of information |
|---|---|---|
| Giving changes people's brain chemistry. | researchers at the University of Oregon | Think about where the information in an article is coming from. This will help you judge the quality of the information. |
| Giving reduces people's stress. | | |
| Giving lowers people's blood pressure. | | |
| Giving makes people live longer. | | |

**E** PAIRS  What is the article about? Retell the most important ideas. Use your own words.

## 4 MAKE IT PERSONAL

What other ways can giving improve your health? 🔍

**A** THINK  When was the last time you helped a stranger? What did you do? How did the person feel? How did you feel? Why did you feel this way?

**B** PAIRS  Share your experiences.

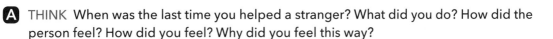

☐ I CAN READ ABOUT THE HEALTH BENEFITS OF GIVING.

**PABLO PIÑEDA**

@PabloP

I was really mad at my bank, but I think I've solved the problem.

## 1 BEFORE YOU WRITE

**A** What problems have you had with a store or bank? How did you resolve them?

**B** Complete the sentences with the words in the box.

| debit | credit |
|---|---|

1. The bank will _____ the money to your account as soon as you put it in.
2. The bank will _____ the money from your account when you spend it.

**C** Read Pablo's email. Why did he write it?

Subject: Loan #521847936

From: Pablo Piñeda    To: customerservice@mybank

Dear Sir or Madam:

I am writing in regard to my loan #521847936. My loan payment of $165 is automatically taken out of my checking account every month, but on April 25 I received a late payment email from you. I confirmed, however, that my checking account was debited on that date for that amount.

I called Customer Service and spoke to Ms. Sara Johnston. She acknowledged that there was a banking error and promised to take care of the problem, stating that the payment would appear on my loan account within 10 business days. However, it is now 14 business days since that phone call, and the payment has still not been credited to my account. In addition, I was charged interest and a late fee.

Would you kindly credit my account and remove the late fee and interest charge? I would also appreciate it if you would send me an email confirmation or have a representative phone me when the error is corrected. Please take care of this as soon as possible. Until now, my loan payments were always credited on time, and I have a good credit history. I'm concerned that this error may affect my credit score.

Thank you for your attention to this matter. Please let me know if any further information is required.

Sincerely,

Pablo Piñeda

**D** Read the email again. Take notes in the chart.

| General problem | |
|---|---|
| More detailed explanation of the problem | |
| Request | |

## 2 FOCUS ON WRITING

Read the Writing Skill. Then reread Pablo's email. Find the examples of polite language in the email that have the same meaning as the less polite language below. Complete the chart.

| Less polite language | Polite language |
|---|---|
| You have to credit my account… | Would you kindly credit my account… |
| You have to send me an email… | |
| Do this right away. | |
| Thanks for taking care of this. | |
| Tell me if you need anything else. | |

**WRITING SKILL**
**Use polite language in a formal email**

Use polite language in a formal email when writing to complain or dispute a problem. It is more effective than using language that demands action. Polite requests usually help you get the results you want. Notice the difference between *Could you please find out how the problem happened?* and *I insist you tell me what happened!*

## 3 PLAN YOUR WRITING

**A** THINK  When did you have a dispute with a company? What was the general problem, what were the details of the problem, and how did you want them to resolve the problem? Draw a chart like the one in 1D.

**B** PAIRS  Talk about the dispute.

*I disputed a charge from my credit card company because they charged me a late fee twice.*

## 4 WRITE

Write an email about a financial charge from a company that you thought was incorrect. Describe the problem and how you want them to resolve it. Include polite language. Use the email in 1C as a model.

## 5 REVISE YOUR WRITING

**A** PAIRS  Exchange emails and read each other's writing.

1. Did your partner clearly state the problem and what he or she wanted done about it? Underline the problem and circle the request.
2. Did your partner use polite language? Check (✓) the examples of polite language.

**Revising tip**
Take a walk and think about the language in your email. If you're writing about a dispute, it's a good idea to step away and calm down before you revise it and send it.

**B** PAIRS  Can your partner improve his or her email? Make suggestions.

## 6 PROOFREAD

Read your email again. Check your
- spelling
- punctuation
- capitalization

# PUT IT TOGETHER

## 1 PRESENTATION PROJECT

**A** ▶02-20 Listen or watch. What is the topic of the presentation?

**B** ▶02-21 Listen or watch again. Answer the questions.

1. Why was Misaki excited by the project?

   _____

2. Who is this product good for?

   _____

3. What did the creator offer to investors?

   _____

**C** Read the presentation skill. How can you get better at this skill?

> **PRESENTATION SKILL**
>
> **Speak with authority**
> Your audience expects you to be an authority on your topic—so, even if you don't feel confident, pretend that you are.

**D** Make your own presentation.

**Step 1** Search the internet for a crowdfunding project that would interest you. Search "**crowdfunding**" plus a hobby or subject that you're interested in.

**Step 2** Prepare a two-minute presentation about the crowdfunding project. Include information about why the product is special and what the creator offers to investors. Bring an item or picture that relates to your project.

**Step 3** Give your presentation to the class. Remember to use the presentation skill. Answer questions and get feedback.

> How did you do? Complete the self-evaluation on page 165.

## 2 REFLECT AND PLAN

**A** Look back through the unit. Check (✓) the things you learned. Highlight the things you need to learn.

**Speaking objectives**
- ☐ Ask about a return policy
- ☐ Discuss taking out a loan
- ☐ Talk about crowdfunding

**Vocabulary**
- ☐ Return policy language
- ☐ Language for loans

**Conversation**
- ☐ Ask questions for clarification

**Pronunciation**
- ☐ Blend past modals

**Listening**
- ☐ Listen for the introduction and conclusion

**Grammar**
- ☐ *As long as, providing (that), unless*
- ☐ Past unreal conditional
- ☐ Connectives to express contrast and surprise

**Reading**
- ☐ Identify sources of information

**Writing**
- ☐ Use polite language in a formal email

**B** What will you do to learn the things you highlighted? For example, use your app, review your Student Book, or do other practice. Make a plan.

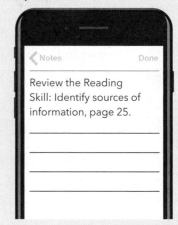

Notes                    Done

Review the Reading Skill: Identify sources of information, page 25.

_____

_____

_____

# 3 HAVE YOU SEEN A DOCTOR?

## LEARNING GOALS

In this unit, you
- ⊗ describe how you feel and ask for advice
- ⊗ describe injuries and report advice
- ⊗ talk about medical research
- ⊗ read about the pros and cons of an issue
- ⊗ write a summary

## GET STARTED

**A** Read the unit title and learning goals.

**B** Look at the photo. What's going on?

**C** Now read Gina's message. What is she worried about? Why?

**GINA CLARK**
@GinaC

A lot of people in my office have the flu. I have so much work to do I can't get sick now.

# DESCRIBE HOW YOU FEEL AND ASK FOR ADVICE

**GINA CLARK**
@GinaC

Not feeling well today. Woke up with a sore throat and a headache.

## 1 VOCABULARY  Flu symptoms

**A** Look at the poster. What are some common flu symptoms? What advice does the poster give?

**B** ▶03-01 Listen. Then listen and repeat.

### Know Your **Flu Symptoms**  How do you know if you have the flu?

**Do you feel...**

| weak and **fatigued**, | **nauseous**, | **dizzy**, | and/or all **stuffed-up**? |

**Do you have...**

| **a fever**, | the **chills**, | **muscle aches and pains**, | and/or **a runny nose**? |

Other common symptoms include a cough, a sore throat, and a headache. If you have some or all of these symptoms, talk to your doctor right away. Don't go back to work or school until you are better!

**C** ▶03-02 Listen. Which flu symptom does each speaker have? Write words from **1B**.

1. _____  3. _____  5. _____  7. _____

2. _____  4. _____  6. _____  8. _____

**D** PAIRS  Brainstorm the best ways to treat the symptoms in **1B**.

## 2 GRAMMAR  Giving and asking for advice: Review and expand

Use the modal verbs *should*, *had better*, and *ought to* to give direct advice. Use the structure *if I were (someone else)* to give less direct advice.

| Giving Advice: Modals | | | Giving Advice: *If I were (someone else)* | | |
|---|---|---|---|---|---|
| **Subject** | **Modal** | **Advice** | ***If I were*** | **(someone else)** | **Result clause** |
| You | should (not) | | | you, | I'd stay home. |
| Linda | had better (not) | stay home. | If I were | Linda, | I wouldn't stay home. |
| Those kids | ought to | | | those kids, | |
| **Asking for Advice: Modals** | | | **Asking for Advice: *If you were me*** | | |
| Should I stay home? | | | Would you stay home if you were me? | | |
| What should I do? | | | What would you do if you were me? | | |

**Notes**
- *Should* and *had better* are more common than *ought to*.
- Do not use *ought to* or *had better* for questions.

**>> FOR PRACTICE, GO TO PAGE 131**

# 3 PRONUNCIATION

**A** ▶03-03 Read and listen to the pronunciation note.

> **Link consonant and vowel sounds**
>
> Link a word that ends in a consonant sound to a word that begins with a vowel sound:
> *I feel a bit nauseous.*
> Final consonants linked to vowels are easier to hear.

**B** ▶03-04 Listen. Notice the linking between final consonants and beginning vowels. Then listen and repeat.

1. You'd better take it easy for a few days.
2. I'd stay home if I were you.
3. Elena's back aches and she feels a bit nauseous.
4. If I were you, I'd make an appointment with an eye doctor.

**C** ▶03-05 Listen. Underline the linking between final consonants and beginning vowels. Then listen again and repeat.

1. Michael looks a little under the weather.
2. When Ana woke up, she had a sore throat and felt exhausted.
3. Ask Elena to pick Alex up as soon as she can.
4. Forget about going out tonight. You have a bad cough.

# 4 CONVERSATION

**A** ▶03-06 Listen or watch. What are Michael and Gina talking about?

**B** ▶03-07 Listen or watch again. Answer the questions.

1. Why hasn't Gina seen a doctor yet?
2. Why does Michael think Gina should see a doctor?
3. How is Gina going to get home?
4. Why is Gina concerned at the end of the conversation?

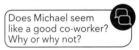

> Does Michael seem like a good co-worker? Why or why not?

**C** ▶03-08 FOCUS ON LANGUAGE Listen or watch. Complete the conversation.

**Michael:** Hey, Gina. How's it going? Oh, are you all right?

**Gina:** Not really. For a second there, I felt a little _____ .

**Michael:** Uh-oh. Maybe _____ take it easy for a few minutes. Is there anything I can get you? Water?

**Gina:** No, that's OK. I think I'm just coming down with something. This morning, I had a sore throat and a headache, and now, I'm feeling weak and a bit _____ .

# 5 TRY IT YOURSELF

**A** THINK Imagine that you're sick. Take notes about your symptoms.

**B** ROLE PLAY Student A: You notice that your co-worker looks sick. Ask what's wrong and give advice. Student B: Respond. Use the conversation in 4C as an example.

**C** EVALUATE Tell the class about your partner's symptoms and the advice you gave. Do your classmates think you gave good advice?

■ I CAN DESCRIBE HOW I FEEL AND ASK FOR ADVICE.

**GINA CLARK**
@GinaC

You won't believe this. Now I'm at the hospital with my sister. What a day!

 **1 VOCABULARY** Injuries and treatments

 **A** ▶03-09 **Listen. Then listen and repeat.**

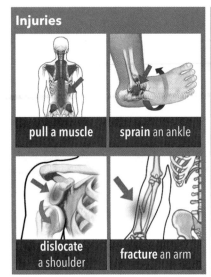

**Injuries**

| pull a muscle | sprain an ankle |
| dislocate a shoulder | fracture an arm |

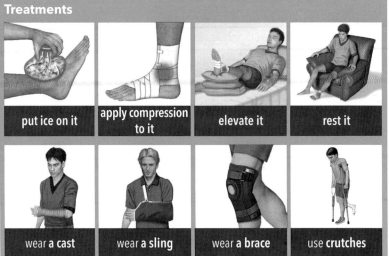

**Treatments**

| put ice on it | apply compression to it | elevate it | rest it |
| wear a cast | wear a sling | wear a brace | use crutches |

**B** **PAIRS** Which of these injuries have you or someone you know had? How did you or someone you know treat them? Use words from 1A.

## 2 GRAMMAR  Reporting advice: Review and expand

Common verbs for reporting advice include *say, tell, recommend,* and *suggest.*
***Say*** and ***tell*** can be followed by an infinitive.

| Subject | Verb | Object | (*Not*) | Infinitive | |
|---|---|---|---|---|---|
| The doctor | said | | (not) | to take | medicine. |
| | told | me | | to go | to work. |

***Say*** and ***tell*** can also be followed by a ***that*** clause.

| Subject 1 | Verb | Object | (*That*) | Subject 2 | |
|---|---|---|---|---|---|
| The doctor | said | | (that) | I | shouldn't go to work. |
| | told | me | | | |

**Note:** Do not use an object after *said,* but always use an object after *told.*

***Suggest*** and ***recommend*** can be followed by a ***that*** clause.

| Subject 1 | Verb | (*That*) | Subject 2 | Base form of the verb | |
|---|---|---|---|---|---|
| The doctor | suggested | (that) | I | take | some medicine. |

**Note:** With *suggest* and *recommend,* use the base form of the verb in the *that* clause for all subjects: *The doctor suggested/recommended that he/she (not) **take** the medicine.*

***Suggest*** and ***recommend*** can also be followed by a gerund.

| Subject | Verb | (*Not*) | Gerund | |
|---|---|---|---|---|
| The doctor | recommended | (not) | going | to work. |

**>> FOR PRACTICE, GO TO PAGE 132**

# 3 CONVERSATION SKILL

**A** ▶03-10 Read the conversation skill. Listen. Notice that Speaker B responds to bad news by showing concern and asking a question.

1. A: John was just taken to the hospital.
   B: Oh, no. What happened?
2. A: There was a big accident today.
   B: That's terrible. Did anyone get hurt?

**B** PAIRS Practice the conversations.

## Respond to bad news

Respond to bad news by showing concern and asking for more information.

| Showing concern | Asking for more information |
|---|---|
| *Oh, no.* | *What happened?* |
| *That's terrible.* | *Is everyone OK?* |
| *I'm sorry to hear that.* | *What did the doctor say?* |
| *Uh-oh.* | *Did anyone get hurt?* |

# 4 CONVERSATION

**A** ▶03-11 Listen or watch. Why does Gina call Michael?

**B** ▶03-12 Listen or watch again. Answer the questions.

1. What injury did Michael have a couple of years ago?
2. What was the treatment for Michael's injury?
3. How is Gina feeling now?
4. Is Gina going to go to work tomorrow? Why or why not?

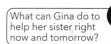

What can Gina do to help her sister right now and tomorrow?

**C** ▶03-13 FOCUS ON LANGUAGE Listen or watch. Complete the conversation.

> **Michael:** What happened to your sister?
>
> **Gina:** She fell on the stairs going up to my house and hurt her ankle. It looked really bad, so I brought her to the hospital right away.
>
> **Michael:** _____ ! Has she seen a doctor yet?
>
> **Gina:** Yeah, she had X-rays, and the doctor told her it's just _____ . It's not fractured or broken.
>
> **Michael:** That's good.
>
> **Gina:** He just _____ that she needs to stay off it as much as possible.

# 5 TRY IT YOURSELF

**A** THINK What injury have you or someone you know had that resulted in a visit to the doctor? Complete the chart.

| | |
|---|---|
| Who was injured? | |
| What was the injury? | |
| How did the injury happen? | |
| What did the doctor say? | |

**B** ROLE PLAY Student A: Tell your partner about the injury. Student B: Respond to the bad news and ask about the doctor's advice. Use the conversation in 4C as an example.

**C** REPORT Tell the class about the injury and advice your partner talked about.

■ I CAN DESCRIBE INJURIES AND REPORT ADVICE.

### GINA CLARK
@GinaC

I just saw a talk about microbes. Did you know that some of them might actually be good for us?

## 1 BEFORE YOU LISTEN

**A** What do you know about microbes, such as viruses and bacteria?

**B** ▶03-14 VOCABULARY Listen. Then listen and repeat.

> **a microbe:** an extremely small living creature that cannot be seen without a microscope
> **a cell:** the smallest part of a living thing
> **existence:** being present or real
> **an antiseptic:** a chemical substance that prevents a wound from becoming infected
> **a vaccine:** a medicine that stops you from getting a disease
> **the gut:** the tube in your body through which food passes
> **digest:** to change food in the stomach to a form your body can use
> **an immune system:** the system by which your body protects itself from disease
> **bloodstream:** blood as it flows around the body
> **sterile:** completely clean and not containing any bacteria

**C** Complete the sentences with words from 1B.

1. Donuts are not good for you because it takes a long time to _____ them.
2. The operating room in the hospital needs to be completely _____ .
3. Your body is made of millions of _____ .
4. Every year, many people get a(n) _____ to prevent the flu.
5. We used a microscope to look at the _____ living in pond water.
6. I never get sick. I think I have a strong _____ .
7. You should put some _____ on that wound so it doesn't get infected.
8. They use a needle to put medicine directly into your _____ .
9. We didn't know about the _____ of microbes until we built microscopes.
10. Eating good food is important for the health of your _____ .

## 2 GRAMMAR  *Not only…but also*

We use *not only…but also* to emphasize that two things are true. The same grammatical form should follow each phrase.

|  |  | **Noun** |  | **Noun** |
|---|---|---|---|---|
| Our bodies contain | not only | viruses | but also | bacteria. |
|  |  | **Prepositional phrase** |  | **Prepositional phrase** |
| Microbes interact | not only | with our human cells | but also | with each other. |
|  |  | **Adjective** |  | **Adjective** |
| They are | not only | helpful | but also | necessary. |

Notes
- We sometimes leave out *also*: *They are not only helpful but necessary.*
- We don't use a comma to separate *not only* and *but also* unless they connect two independent clauses.

**>> FOR PRACTICE, GO TO PAGE 133**

# 3 LISTENING

David Cruz | TSW Global Speaker Program
**Unit 3: The Microbes Within**

**A** ▶03-15 Listen or watch. What is the main idea of the talk?

**B** ▶03-16 Read the Listening Skill. Listen or watch again. There are three main sections between the introduction and conclusion. What is the topic of each of those sections?

**C** ▶03-17 Listen or watch again. Answer the questions.

1. How many cells in the human body are actually microbes?

   _____

2. What did Edward Jenner do?

   _____

3. How do microbes help babies?

   _____

4. When can helpful bacteria become harmful?

   _____

5. What do scientists still want to learn about microbes?

   _____

> **LISTENING SKILL  Listen for topics**
>
> Most talks are organized into sections that focus on a particular topic. This helps the listener follow along and understand the speaker's main idea.

**D** VOCABULARY EXPANSION  Read each sentence from the talk. What do the underlined expressions mean?

1. About two hundred years later, scientists began to make <u>breakthroughs</u> in understanding how microbes cause diseases and used these discoveries to fight them.

   _____

2. We use <u>antimicrobial</u> sprays to clean our kitchens and antimicrobial soap to wash our skin.

   _____

3. These are early days in this exciting field, and we don't have a lot of <u>definitive answers</u> yet.

   _____

**E** PAIRS  Compare your answers in 3D.

# 4 DISCUSSION

**A** THINK  How do people protect themselves from harmful microbes? Complete the chart.

| food | cook meat, wash vegetables, |
| --- | --- |
| water | |
| home | |
| wounds/skin care | |
| flu/cold viruses | |
| insect-borne diseases | |

**B** DISCUSS  In groups, share your ideas from 4A. Are there areas where you think people may be *too* careful about microbes? Do you know of anything people can do to try to increase the number of "good" microbes in their bodies?

**C** REPORT  Tell the class about what you and your group discussed.

☐ I CAN TALK ABOUT MEDICAL RESEARCH.

# READ ABOUT THE PROS AND CONS OF AN ISSUE

**GINA CLARK**
@GinaC

Did you know that dogs can detect cancer? You'll be amazed by what else they can do!

## 1 BEFORE YOU READ

**A** PAIRS How do dogs help people?

**B** ▶03-18 VOCABULARY Listen. Then listen and repeat. Do you know these words?

| cancer | detect | a seizure | a sensor | identify | a ward | a device |

**>> FOR DEFINITIONS AND PRACTICE, GO TO PAGE 133**

## 2 READ

**A** PREVIEW Read the title and look at the photo. What do you think the article will be about?

**B** ▶03-19 Read and listen to the article. Was your prediction correct?

## Could a Dog Save Your Life?

If a dog could talk, what would it say? Besides asking you for food and walks, it might also suggest that you visit your doctor, maybe just in time to save your life!

This was the case for one woman in England in
5 1989. Her dog kept sniffing a mole, or brown spot, on her leg. The dog even tried to bite the mole off. Concerned, the woman went to see her doctor, who removed the mole and discovered that it was a melanoma, a deadly type of skin cancer.

10 Since then, researchers have determined that dogs can detect medical problems other than cancer, too. For example, dogs are able to notice changes in the blood sugar of people who have diabetes, giving these people more time to treat themselves before they have
15 a seizure. Dogs can also locate dangerous bacteria in hospitals so that staff members have the chance to get rid of the bacteria before patients get sick.

Dogs clearly have an amazing ability to detect things, so what's their secret? It's their incredible sense of smell.
20 Dogs have around 300 million smelling sensors, while we have just five or six million. This means that dogs can smell much better than we can, enabling them to notice small changes in our bodies and health that we can't.

Because of this remarkable ability, researchers are
25 eager to find out just how good dogs can be at detecting medical problems. So far, they have learned that there are several advantages to using dogs instead of other detection methods and devices. To begin with, dogs don't make a lot of mistakes. In a study in
30 England, a dog was able to identify cancer 95% of the time. Second, dogs work fast. A dog in the Netherlands checked an entire hospital ward for dangerous bacteria in just ten minutes. It would have taken scientists three to five days to do the same thing. Finally, dogs can
35 make the detection process easier and less painful for patients. Who wouldn't want to be checked by a friendly dog instead of going through a complicated and possibly painful test?

However, there are still some disadvantages to using
40 medical detection dogs. For one thing, they are very expensive to train. It can cost tens of thousands of dollars to train just one dog. In addition, it takes a long time to train them. It took two years to train dogs that were used to detect cancer during a study in Japan.
45 Furthermore, dogs aren't always easy to work with. They aren't machines, so they sometimes get tired and distracted, and they need rewards and breaks to keep them focused.

Because of these drawbacks, we might not see dogs
50 in every hospital in the near future, but they could still help us improve our medical detection processes. Right now, researchers are trying to determine exactly how dogs can detect things like cancer and bacteria. If they can figure this out, they might be able to make an
55 electronic device that could work just like a dog's nose. Then we would still have dogs to thank when doctors warn us about a serious medical problem in advance.

# 3 CHECK YOUR UNDERSTANDING

**A** Read the article again. What is the main idea?

**B** Answer the questions, according to the article.

1. What medical problems can dogs detect?

   _____

2. How can they detect these problems?

   _____

3. What are researchers trying to learn about medical detection dogs?

   _____

4. What kind of device would researchers like to make?

   _____

**C** CLOSE READING Reread lines 20-23 in the article. Then circle the correct answers.

1. In line 21, why does the writer use the word *just*?
   a. to emphasize that people have a lot of smelling sensors
   b. to emphasize that dogs have more smelling sensors than people
   c. to emphasize that we might get more smelling sensors in the future
2. How is the second sentence connected to the first?
   a. It introduces a counterargument.
   b. It gives a list of examples.
   c. It shows a result.

**D** Read the Reading Skill. Complete the sentences with the words from the article. Then complete the chart with the pros and cons.

| Pros | Cons |
|---|---|
| So far, they have learned that there are several _____ to using dogs instead of other detection methods and devices. | However, there are still some _____ to using medical detection dogs. |
| 1. | 1. |
| 2. | 2. |
| 3. | 3. |

> **READING SKILL**
> **Identify pros and cons**
>
> Writers often use key words to introduce the pros and cons of something. Look for pairs of words like *advantages / disadvantages*, *benefits / drawbacks*, and *upsides / downsides*.

**E** PAIRS What is the article about? Retell the most important ideas. Use your own words.

How are dogs helping people near to you?

# 4 MAKE IT PERSONAL

**A** THINK Do you think that dogs or other animals should be used to help people despite the drawbacks? Complete the chart.

| Pros of animals helping people | Cons of animals helping people |
|---|---|
|  |  |

**B** DISCUSS In small groups, share your ideas. Do most people agree?

☐ I CAN READ ABOUT THE PROS AND CONS OF AN ISSUE.

**GINA CLARK**

@GinaC

Can't get that article about medical detection dogs out of my mind!

## 1 BEFORE YOU WRITE

**A** What do you remember about the article "Could a Dog Save Your Life?" on page 36?

**B** Read the summary of the article. Did you remember everything correctly?

> **Summary of "Could a Dog Save Your Life?"**
>
> According to researchers, dogs have an amazing ability to detect many medical problems, including cancer. Dogs can identify these problems because of their fantastic sense of smell. Researchers have learned that medical detection dogs are accurate, fast, and make the experience smoother for patients. However, medical detection dogs take a lot of time and money to train, and they are not always as reliable as machines. In the future, medical detection dogs might not work in hospitals, but they could still help us to get better at detecting medical problems.

## 2 FOCUS ON WRITING

**A** Read the Writing Skill. Then reread the full article and the summary. Is the summary good? Check (✓) the items in the writing skill box that make the summary good.

> **WRITING SKILL Write a good summary**
>
> A summary is a short text that provides the main ideas of a longer text. A good summary:
> - ☐ is written in your own words
> - ☐ has only information found in the original text
> - ☐ includes only the original author's point of view
> - ☐ has only the main ideas from the original text
> - ☐ includes expressions for reporting the text's ideas, such as *According to…* and *As the article explains…*

**B** In the full article, find and underline the main idea that matches each of these sentences from the summary.

| Summary sentences |
|---|
| 1. According to researchers, dogs have an amazing ability to detect many medical problems, including cancer. |
| 2. Dogs can identify these problems because of their fantastic sense of smell. |
| 3. Researchers have learned that medical detection dogs are accurate, fast, and make the experience smoother for patients. |
| 4. However, medical detection dogs take a lot of time and money to train, and they are not always as reliable as machines. |
| 5. In the future, medical detection dogs might not work in hospitals, but they could still help us to get better at detecting medical problems. |

**C** Match the wording in the original article with the wording in the summary that expresses the same idea.

Dogs:

___ 1. have around 300 million smelling sensors

___ 2. make the process easier and less painful

___ 3. sometimes get tired and distracted

___ 4. don't make mistakes

a. are not always as reliable

b. are accurate

c. have a fantastic sense of smell

d. make the experience smoother

# 3 PLAN YOUR WRITING

**A** THINK Read the article "Reaching the Peak" on page 155. Underline the main ideas in the article. Then complete the chart using your own words.

| Main idea in the first paragraph | Main idea in the second paragraph | Main idea in the third paragraph | Main idea in the fourth paragraph | Main idea in the last paragraph |
|---|---|---|---|---|
|  |  |  |  |  |

**B** PAIRS Compare your chart with your partner's. Discuss any differences.

We both have written the same thing about paragraph 1, but we have different information for paragraph 2...

# 4 WRITE

Write a summary of the article "Reaching the Peak." Remember to use only your own words and the information from the original article. Include expressions for reporting the article's ideas. Use the summary in 1B as a model.

# 5 REVISE YOUR WRITING

**A** PAIRS Exchange summaries and read each other's writing.

1. Did your partner clearly summarize the article in his or her own words?
2. Does the summary have only information found in the original article?
3. Does the summary include only the original author's point of view?
4. Does the summary have only the main ideas from the original article?
5. Does the summary include expressions for reporting the article's ideas?

**Revising tip**

Compare your summary to the original text line by line and paragraph by paragraph. This way you can confirm that you included all the main ideas.

**B** PAIRS Can your partner improve his or her summary? Make suggestions.

# 6 PROOFREAD

Read your summary again. Check your
- spelling
- punctuation
- capitalization

■ I CAN WRITE A SUMMARY.

# PUT IT TOGETHER

## 1 PRESENTATION PROJECT

**A** ▶03-20 Listen or watch. What is the topic of the presentation?

**B** ▶03-21 Listen or watch again. Answer the questions.

1. What is the name of the app?

   _____

2. How does the app improve people's health?

   _____

3. What three features does the app have?

   _____

**C** Read the presentation skill. Did you know about this skill?

**D** Make your own presentation.

**Step 1** Choose an app or innovation that has been designed to help people improve their health. Create a graph or chart related to the app or innovation. Remember to use the presentation skill.

> ### PRESENTATION SKILL
> **Keep graphics simple**
> Do not distract audience members with unnecessary words on your visual aids.

**Step 2** Prepare a two-minute presentation about the app or innovation. Include information about what the app or innovation does and how it works. Bring the chart or graph that is related to it.

**Step 3** Give your presentation to the class. Answer questions and get feedback.

## 2 REFLECT AND PLAN

> How did you do? Complete the self-evaluation on page 165.

**A** Look back through the unit. Check (✓) the things you learned. Highlight the things you need to learn.

**Speaking objectives**
- ☐ Describe how you feel and ask for advice
- ☐ Describe injuries and report advice
- ☐ Talk about medical research

**Vocabulary**
- ☐ Flu symptoms
- ☐ Injuries and treatments

**Conversation**
- ☐ Respond to bad news

**Pronunciation**
- ☐ Link consonant and vowel sounds

**Listening**
- ☐ Listen for topics

**Grammar**
- ☐ Giving and asking for advice
- ☐ Reporting advice
- ☐ *Not only...but also*

**Reading**
- ☐ Identify pros and cons

**Writing**
- ☐ Write a good summary

**B** What will you do to learn the things you highlighted? For example, use your app, review your Student Book, or do other practice. Make a plan.

Notes — Done

In the app, do the Lesson 2 Grammar activities: Reporting advice

# 4 ARE YOU DOING ANYTHING SPECIAL?

## LEARNING GOALS

In this unit, you
- ⊘ talk about park rules
- ⊘ talk about outdoor activities
- ⊘ discuss how to help the environment
- ⊘ read a travel website
- ⊘ write a persuasive argument

## GET STARTED

**A** Read the unit title and learning goals.

**B** Look at the photo. What's going on?

**C** Now read Oscar's message. How does he feel about hiking?

OSCAR BLANCO
@OscarB

Went hiking in the mountains last weekend. Time spent among the trees is never time wasted.

## OSCAR BLANCO
@OscarB

I got really mad at these other hikers on the trail. Some people just have no respect for nature.

## 1 VOCABULARY Park rules

**A** ▶04-01 Listen. Then listen and repeat.

Do not litter.

Do not leave fires unattended.

Do not make excessive noise.

Do not feed the wildlife.

Keep pets on a leash.

Stay on the trails.

Store food in animal-proof containers.

Leave the park before dark.

**B** ▶04-02 Listen. Circle the rule that is being broken.

1. Stay on the trails. / Leave the park before dark.
2. Keep pets on a leash. / Do not make excessive noise.
3. Stay on the trails. / Store food in animal-proof containers.
4. Leave the park before dark. / Do not make excessive noise.
5. Do not litter. / Do not feed the wildlife.
6. Store food in animal-proof containers. / Keep pets on a leash.
7. Do not feed the wildlife. / Do not leave fires unattended.
8. Do not leave fires unattended. / Do not litter.

**C** PAIRS What could happen if people don't follow the rules in 1A?

## 2 GRAMMAR *Be supposed to*

We use *be supposed to* and the base form of the verb to talk about rules and expectations.

| Subject | Be | (Not) | Supposed to | Base form of the verb | |
|---------|-----|-------|-------------|----------------------|-----|
| I | am / was | | | | |
| You | are / were | (not) | supposed to | stay | on the trails. |
| She | is / was | | | | |

**Notes**

- Use *be supposed to* only with the simple present or simple past.
- Affirmative statements in the past suggest that something didn't happen:
  *She was supposed to stay on the trails.* (But she didn't.)
- Negative statements in the past suggest that something did happen:
  *She wasn't supposed to feed the animals.* (But she did.)

>> FOR PRACTICE, GO TO PAGE 134

# 3 PRONUNCIATION

**A** ▶04-03 Read and listen to the pronunciation note.

**B** ▶04-04 Listen. Notice how *supposed to* is pronounced. Then listen and repeat.

/səpouztə/
You're supposed to stay on the trails.
You're not supposed to litter.

/spouztə/
You're supposed to leave before dark.
You're not supposed to feed the animals.

**C** PAIRS Talk about rules at home, school, or work. Use *supposed to.*

# 4 CONVERSATION

**A** ▶04-05 Listen or watch. What are Oscar and Elena talking about?

**B** ▶04-06 Listen or watch again. Answer the questions.
1. Where did some hikers leave their trash?
2. What are hikers supposed to do with their trash?
3. What did Oscar see at the end of the trail?
4. What made the whole trip worthwhile for Oscar?

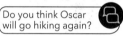
Do you think Oscar will go hiking again?

**C** ▶04-07 FOCUS ON LANGUAGE Listen or watch. Complete the conversation.

Elena: Hey, Oscar. I heard you went hiking last weekend. How was it?

Oscar: Well, the mountains were really beautiful, but some of the people there really made me mad.

Elena: What do you mean?

Oscar: Well, this other group of hikers went off into a conservation area to take selfies. You're _____ to stay on the _____ .

Elena: I guess they weren't aware of the rules.

Oscar: Yeah, or they just didn't care. There were signs everywhere telling people to keep out, but they went in anyway.

# 5 TRY IT YOURSELF

**A** THINK Think of a time when someone broke the rules in a park or other outdoor area. What did the person do? Take notes.

**B** PAIRS Student A: Tell your story about someone who broke the rules. Use the information in 5A. Student B: Ask questions. Use the conversation in 4C as an example.

**C** REPORT Tell the class about your partner's story. Who had the worst experience? What rules were broken more often than others?

■ I CAN TALK ABOUT PARK RULES.

# TALK ABOUT OUTDOOR ACTIVITIES

## OSCAR BLANCO
@OscarB

Some of my co-workers take such adventurous vacations. I need to make time for things like that.

## 1 VOCABULARY Outdoor activities

**A** ▶04-08 **Listen. Then listen and repeat.**

| soak in a hot spring | bike along mountain cliffs | raft on the rapids | paddleboard along the shore |
| zipline through a rain forest | snorkel along a coral reef | ride horseback on the beach | take a boat to a waterfall |

**B** ▶04-09 **Listen. Which activity is the speaker describing? Write words from 1A.**

1. _____
2. _____
3. _____
4. _____
5. _____
6. _____
7. _____
8. _____

**C** PAIRS Which activities in 1A would you try? Which wouldn't you try? Why?

## 2 GRAMMAR Future continuous

We use the future continuous to talk about actions that will be in progress at a specific time in the future.

### Statements

| Time phrase | Subject | Will / won't | Be | Present participle | |
|---|---|---|---|---|---|
| Next week, | I | will / won't | be | soaking | in a hot spring. |
| | they | will / won't | | | |

### Questions

| | Will | Subject | Be | Present participle | | Time phrase |
|---|---|---|---|---|---|---|
| | Will | you | be | soaking | in a hot spring | next week? |
| What | will | she | | doing | | next week? |

### Notes

- The future continuous is often used to talk about future plans and intentions.
- Only action verbs can be used as the present participle in the future continuous: *walking, running, snorkeling, riding,* etc. NOT: *be, know, sound, belong, like,* etc.

>> FOR PRACTICE, GO TO PAGE 135

## 3 CONVERSATION SKILL

**A** ▶04-10 Read the conversation skill. Listen. Notice how Speaker B keeps the conversation going by asking a question.

1. A: I'm thinking about taking a long trip next year.
   B: Where do you want to go?

2. A: We hiked up to the top of the volcano.
   B: Did it take a long time?

**B** ▶04-11 Listen. Circle the question you hear.

1. a. Where are you going?
   b. Will you be going to Machu Picchu?
2. a. Are you excited?
   b. Where are they going to take you?

## 4 CONVERSATION

**A** ▶04-12 Listen or watch. What does Elena tell Oscar about?

**B** ▶04-13 Listen or watch again. Answer the questions.

1. How long will Elena be in Costa Rica?
2. Who is Elena going to Costa Rica with?
3. What will Elena be doing during her vacation?
4. What do Elena and Oscar agree about at the end of the conversation?

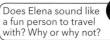
Does Elena sound like a fun person to travel with? Why or why not?

**C** ▶04-14 FOCUS ON LANGUAGE Listen or watch. Complete the conversation.

> Oscar: I saw your email about taking some time off. Are you going anywhere special?
>
> Elena: Haven't you heard? By this time next week, my friends and I will be _____ through the rain forest, or maybe snorkeling along a(n) _____ .
>
> Oscar: Whoa, _____ are you going to do all those things?
>
> Elena: Costa Rica. We're flying in to the capital and then driving out to the coast.
>
> Oscar: Cool!

## 5 TRY IT YOURSELF

**A** THINK Imagine you are taking a vacation next month. Complete the chart.

| Where I'll be going | What I'll be doing |
| --- | --- |
|  |  |

**B** PAIRS Student A: Talk about your vacation plans. Student B: Maintain the conversation by asking questions. Use the conversation in 4C as an example.

**C** REPORT Tell the class about your partner's plans. Who is planning the most interesting vacation?

■ I CAN TALK ABOUT OUTDOOR ACTIVITIES.

# LESSON 3 — DISCUSS HOW TO HELP THE ENVIRONMENT

## OSCAR BLANCO
@OscarB

So much bad news about the environment. The problems seem so big. Watching this talk showed me how one person can make a difference.

## 1 BEFORE YOU LISTEN

**A** Have you ever done something to help the environment? What did you do?

**B** ▶04-15 VOCABULARY Listen. Then listen and repeat.

> **climate change**: important changes to worldwide weather
> **contaminated**: containing dangerous or harmful things
> **a sample**: a small amount of something that shows what the rest is like
> **a glacier**: a large mass of ice that moves slowly over an area of land
> **urban**: relating to a town or city
> **filter**: to clean a liquid or gas by passing it through something
> **content**: happy and satisfied

**C** Complete the sentences with words from 1B.

1. They decided to move from the countryside to a more _____ area, where they could have more opportunities for work and education.
2. When a _____ melts, it causes sea levels to rise.
3. After cleaning up all the trash on the beach, he went home tired but _____ .
4. The scientists collected a _____ of the water to check for pollution.
5. The earth can get warmer or colder because of _____ .
6. Hikers need to _____ river water to make it clean and safe to drink.
7. It is not safe to drink _____ water.

## 2 GRAMMAR Reduced restrictive relative clauses

In restrictive relative clauses, the relative pronoun can be left out when it is the object of the relative clause.

| Main clause | Restrictive relative clause | | | |
|---|---|---|---|---|
| | Object pronoun | Subject | Verb | |
| Scientists developed special fins | (that) | surfers | can attach | to their surfboards. |
| The scientist | (who) | we | met | at the conference won an award. |

**Notes**
- The relative pronoun is often left out in speech and informal writing.
- The relative pronoun cannot be left out when it is the subject of the clause:
  *Divers who study the underwater environment are called scientific divers.*

>> FOR PRACTICE, GO TO PAGE 136

## 3 LISTENING

**A** ▶04-16 Listen or watch. What is the main idea of the talk?

**B** ▶04-17 Read the Listening Skill. Listen or watch again. Complete the sentences with the words and phrases that identify causes and effects.

1. Climate change is _____ the earth to get warmer.
2. Our air and water are becoming contaminated _____ pollution.
3. Others are monitoring and restoring coral reefs that have been damaged _____ rising ocean temperatures.

TSW MEDIA

Adriana Lopez | TSW Global Speaker Program
**Unit 4: Making a Difference**

**LISTENING SKILL**
**Listen for cause and effect**

Listen for words and phrases like *due to, cause, effect, because of, as a result of, in turn, since, thus,* and *so* to identify causes and effects.

**C** ▶04-18 Listen or watch again. Answer the questions.

1. How is Jill working with scientists?
   _____
2. What else is Jill doing to help the environment?
   _____
3. What is Tim doing to help the environment?
   _____
4. How can other people get involved in helping the environment?
   _____

**D** VOCABULARY EXPANSION  Read each sentence from the talk. What do the underlined expressions mean?

1. <u>Let's face it</u>—our planet is in trouble.
   _____
2. Lots of people like Jill are <u>teaming up</u> with scientists to help the environment.
   _____
3. They're ordinary people, just like you and me. But they're <u>pitching in</u> to make the world a better place.
   _____

**E** PAIRS  Compare answers in 3D.

## 4 DISCUSSION

**A** THINK  What are some environmental problems where you live or that you know about? How could you or other people help to solve them? Complete the chart.

| Environmental problems | Solutions |
|---|---|
|  |  |
|  |  |

**B** PAIRS  Discuss the problems and solutions.

**C** COMPARE  Share the problems and solutions with the class. Which problems are the biggest? Are there any problems that everyone could help with?

☐ I CAN DISCUSS HOW TO HELP THE ENVIRONMENT.

**OSCAR BLANCO**
@OscarB

Can't wait to plan my next vacation! So hard to choose where to go.

## 1 BEFORE YOU READ

**A**   PAIRS   Where do you like to go on vacation? What do you like to do there?

**B**   ▶04-19 VOCABULARY   Listen. Then listen and repeat. Do you know these words?

| exotic | luxury | gourmet | world-class | cuisine | stroll | rugged |

>> **FOR DEFINITIONS AND PRACTICE, GO TO PAGE 136**

## 2 READ

**A**   PREVIEW   Read the title and look at the pictures. What do you think the website is about?

**B**   ▶04-20 Read and listen to the information on the website. Was your prediction correct?

---

CALL NOW: 1 800 555 5555    LOCATION    SEARCH

# ADVENTURES ONLY TRAVEL

**HAVE THE ADVENTURE OF A LIFETIME IN SOUTH AMERICA**

Tired of the same old guided bus tours that take you from one crowded tourist attraction to another? Want more excitement and adventure from your trips?

Then let Adventures Only Travel plan your next vacation. We offer exotic
5   adventures, not just tours. Each of our adventures is designed to give you an experience you'll never forget.

**OUR ADVENTURE OPTIONS**

In addition to our Classic Beach Adventure and Latin Food Adventure, we are pleased to offer you two new South American adventures this year.

10   **THE CITY ADVENTURE: BUENOS AIRES**

Discover the beauty of Buenos Aires, the capital and heart of Argentina, and travel in comfort and style on this ten-day city adventure. Enjoy five-star, luxury accommodations and gourmet food as you
15   get to know the "Paris of the South."

Highlights of this adventure include:

- Tasting world-class cuisine at a *parrilla*—one of the barbecue restaurants famous for their steaks and other grilled meats
20  
- Watching a musical performance at the historic Teatro Colón opera house, considered one of the top ten opera houses in the world
- Strolling down the world's widest avenue, Avenida 9 de Julio, to see the incredible
25   architecture in Buenos Aires
- Shopping on the Calle Florida, a street full of cafés and fantastic shops—take a break to watch the tango dancers and other street performers!

**THE EXTREME OUTDOOR ADVENTURE: PATAGONIA**

30   Journey off the beaten path and explore the wild side of Patagonia in this ten-day extreme outdoor adventure. Sleep under the stars and eat and travel like the locals do as you journey to the end of the world and back.

35   Highlights of this adventure include:

- Climbing to the top of the 2,652-meter-tall active Osorno volcano in Chile
- Hiking across the endless Perito Moreno Glacier in Los Glaciares National Park in
40   southern Argentina
- Rafting the world-famous rapids on the Futaleufú River in Chile, surrounded by the rugged peaks of the Andes Mountains
- Camping overnight in Torres del Paine
45   National Park in Chile—home to a wide range of wild animals, including pumas and foxes

> So what are you waiting for? Contact one of our specialists and start
  your adventure today! We're looking forward to helping you have
50 the vacation of your dreams!

## 3 CHECK YOUR UNDERSTANDING

**A** Read the website again. What is it advertising?

**B** Answer the questions, according to the website.

1. What is special about Adventures Only Travel?

   _____

2. What two new adventures is Adventures Only Travel offering this year?

   _____

3. How are the two new adventures different?

   _____

4. What kind of travelers do you think each new adventure is for? Why?

   _____

**C** CLOSE READING Reread lines 4–6 on the website. Then circle the correct answers.

1. In line 5, why does the writer use the word *just*?
   a. to emphasize that the adventures are the same as other tours
   b. to emphasize that the adventures are more special than tours
   c. to emphasize that the adventures include many kinds of tours
2. How is the second sentence connected to the first sentence?
   a. It explains how the adventures are more special than other tours.
   b. It gives some examples of the different kinds of tours you can take.
   c. It provides some reasons why people no longer like to take tours.

**D** Read the Reading Skill. Then read the examples of hyperbole. Write what you think each one means.

| Hyperbole | Possible meaning |
|---|---|
| an experience you'll never forget | an experience you'll remember for a long time |
| journey to the end of the world and back | |
| the endless Perito Moreno Glacier | |
| the vacation of your dreams | |

> **READING SKILL** Recognize hyperbole
>
> Writers sometimes use exaggerated statements to emphasize something or add humor. They do not expect readers to believe every word in these statements.

**E** PAIRS What is the website about? Retell the most important ideas. Use your own words.

The website is about adventures in South America…

> What other things can you do in Buenos Aires and Patagonia?

## 4 MAKE IT PERSONAL

**A** THINK Which of the adventures on the website would you prefer to take? Why?

**B** PAIRS Compare answers. Do you have the same interests in traveling?

☐ I CAN READ A TRAVEL WEBSITE.

LESSON 5   WRITE A PERSUASIVE ARGUMENT

### OSCAR BLANCO
@OscarB

Started a campaign to stop energy companies from ruining the environment. Read my blog to find out more!

## 1 BEFORE YOU WRITE

**A** What energy sources do you know about? How do they affect the environment?

**B** Complete the sentences with the words in the box.

| release    claim    leak |

1. Some people _____ they can remove all the plastic from the ocean, but we're not sure.
2. Oil continued to _____ from the broken pipe into the river for days.
3. Cars _____ harmful chemicals into the air.

**C** Read Oscar's blog. Does he support fracking? Why or why not?

---

Blog | About | Contact                                            🔍 Search

## Fracking: An Environmental Danger

*About*
*RSS Feed*
*Social Media*
*Recent Posts*
*Archives*
*Email*

In the future, we could run out of traditional sources of energy, such as oil and gas, so people are looking for other ways to get fuel. One of the newest options is a process called fracking. During this process, fracking liquid is used to break open rocks deep underground and release gas and oil into special wells. Supporters of fracking claim that it is necessary because it will provide us with the fuel we need for the future. They also say that it is safe for people and the environment. However, the truth is that fracking is extremely dangerous for the environment and people living and working near fracking sites.

Supporters of fracking argue that fracking doesn't harm the environment as long as it's done properly, but that just isn't true. Fracking liquid contains harmful chemicals. They often leak into the water under the ground during the fracking process. A study by Duke University showed that fracking contaminates water. According to the study, water wells near fracking sites were seventeen times more polluted than other wells.

Fracking supporters also insist that fracking is safe for people. In truth, fracking causes very serious health problems. People drink the polluted water and get sick. A study by two American universities also concluded that people who live and work near fracking sites are more likely to have heart problems and cancer than other people.

In conclusion, fracking is very bad for the environment and people. In the future, we might need to find new sources of energy, but fracking is definitely not the answer.

**Leave a Reply**

Enter your comment here...

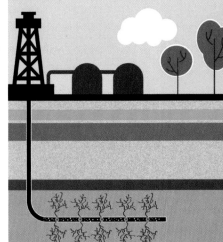

**D** Read the blog again. Did it persuade you that fracking is dangerous? Why or why not?

## 2 FOCUS ON WRITING

Read the Writing Skill. Then reread Oscar's blog. Underline the ways that Oscar introduces opposing arguments. Then complete the chart.

| Main Argument | |
| --- | --- |
| | |
| Opposing Argument 1 | Counterargument 1 |
| Fracking doesn't hurt the environment. | |
| Opposing Argument 2 | Counterargument 2 |
| Fracking is safe for people. | |
| Conclusion | |
| | |

## 3 PLAN YOUR WRITING

**A** THINK  Read the pros and cons of wind turbines. Do you think they are a good way to produce energy? Draw a chart like the one in 2. Include a main argument, opposing arguments, and counterarguments.

| Wind Turbines: Pros and Cons | |
| --- | --- |
| Pros | Cons |
| better for the environment because they are cleaner than other sources of energy | can harm birds, bats, and other wildlife |
| cheaper than other sources of energy | cost a lot to make and install |

**B** PAIRS  Explain why you think wind turbines are a good or bad way to produce energy.

## 4 WRITE

Write a blog either for or against using wind turbines to produce energy. Use the blog in 1C as a model.

**Pre-writing tip**
Research opposing arguments thoroughly. This way you can argue against them clearly and strongly.

## 5 REVISE YOUR WRITING

**A** PAIRS  Exchange blogs and read each other's writing.
1. Did your partner include opposing arguments?
2. Did your partner provide counterarguments with supporting facts?

**B** PAIRS  Can your partner improve his or her blog? Make suggestions.

## 6 PROOFREAD

Read your blog again. Check your
- spelling
- punctuation
- capitalization

■ I CAN WRITE A PERSUASIVE ARGUMENT.

# PUT IT TOGETHER

## 1 PRESENTATION PROJECT

▶ **A** ▶04-21 Listen or watch. What is the topic of the presentation?

▶ **B** ▶04-22 Listen or watch again. Answer the questions.

1. Where is Zhangjiajie National Forest Park?

   _____

2. What does Misaki say is unusual in the park?

   _____

3. What three things can you do there?

   _____

**C** Read the presentation skill. Why is this skill a good idea?

**D** Make your own presentation.

Step 1 Think of a place that is naturally beautiful.

Step 2 Prepare a two-minute presentation about this place. Include where it is, what makes it special or unusual, and what you can do there. Remember to use the presentation skill. Bring a picture that is related to it.

Step 3 Give your presentation to the class. Answer questions and get feedback.

> ### PRESENTATION SKILL
>
> **Give your audience an overview**
> At the beginning of your presentation, list your main points to let audience members know what to expect so that they can follow along better.

## 2 REFLECT AND PLAN

How did you do? Complete the self-evaluation on page 165.

**A** Look back through the unit. Check (✓) the things you learned. Highlight the things you need to learn.

**Speaking objectives**
- ☐ Talk about park rules
- ☐ Talk about outdoor activities
- ☐ Discuss how to help the environment

**Vocabulary**
- ☐ Park rules
- ☐ Outdoor activities

**Conversation**
- ☐ Maintain a conversation by asking questions

**Pronunciation**
- ☐ *Supposed to*

**Listening**
- ☐ Listen for cause and effect

**Grammar**
- ☐ *Be supposed to*
- ☐ Future continuous
- ☐ Reduced restrictive relative clauses

**Reading**
- ☐ Recognize hyperbole

**Writing**
- ☐ Introduce opposing arguments

**B** What will you do to learn the things you highlighted? For example, use your app, review your Student Book, or do other practice. Make a plan.

 Notes                        Done

Review the pronunciation note: *Supposed to*, page 43.

_____

_____

_____

_____

# 5 WHAT SEEMS TO BE THE PROBLEM?

## LEARNING GOALS

In this unit, you
- ⊘ describe technology problems
- ⊘ talk about technology solutions
- ⊘ discuss how technology affects us
- ⊘ read an article about hacking
- ⊘ write a product review

## GET STARTED

**A** Read the unit title and learning goals.

**B** Look at the photo. What's going on?

**C** Now read Michael's message. Where is he going? Why?

MICHAEL STEWART
@MichaelS

Headed to the New York office for a big meeting. Giving an important presentation.

53

## MICHAEL STEWART
@MichaelS

My presentation is about to start.
Hope everything goes smoothly!
Fingers crossed!

## 1 VOCABULARY  Technology problems

**A** Read the ad for computer support. How much time do people waste with technology problems?

**B** ▶05-01 Listen. Then listen and repeat.

**DID YOU KNOW?** On average, people deal with technology problems for more than twenty minutes each day. Are you having frustrating tech problems at work, home, or school?

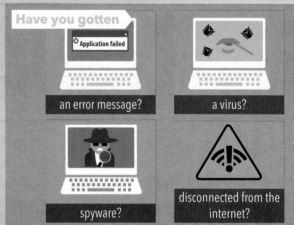

| Has your |  | Have you gotten |  |
|---|---|---|---|
| hard drive crashed? | log-in failed? | an error message? | a virus? |
| battery died? | screen frozen? | spyware? | disconnected from the internet? |

If so, we are here to help! Just give us a call or talk to one of our online support staff members.
**We can help you solve all these problems and many more!**

**C** ▶05-02 Listen. Which technology problem is the speaker describing? Write a word or phrase from 1B.

1. _____      3. _____      5. _____

2. _____      4. _____      6. _____

**D** TAKE A POLL  Who in the class has had these problems? How much time do you think you spend on technology problems every day?

## 2 GRAMMAR  Past perfect continuous

We use the past perfect continuous to show that an activity started in the past and continued up until another point in the past.

| Statements | | | |
|---|---|---|---|
| **Subject** | **Had (not) + been** | **Present participle** | |
| I They | had been | loading | my presentation files when the screen froze. |

| Questions | | | | |
|---|---|---|---|---|
| | **Had** | **Subject** | **Been** | **Present participle** | |
| | Had | you | been | loading | your files when the screen froze? |
| What | had | you | been | doing | when the screen froze? |

**>> FOR PRACTICE, GO TO PAGE 137**

# 3 PRONUNCIATION

**A** ▶05-03 Read and listen to the pronunciation note.

**B** ▶05-04 Listen. Notice how the final consonants are pronounced. Then listen and repeat.

Final consonant + Different beginning consonant
blan**k** page, lap**t**op, pa**ss**word, te**ch** support

Final consonant + Same beginning consonant
suppor**t** team, har**d** drive, hal**f**-finished, bi**g** game

Final /st/ + Different beginning consonant
las~~t~~ night, nex~~t~~ problem, firs~~t~~ computer

**Link final consonants to beginning consonants**

In English, final consonants are usually shorter than beginning consonants, especially when they are followed by words beginning with a consonant.

1. **Final consonant + Different beginning consonant**
   Pronounce both consonant sounds. Keep the final consonant short and say the next word immediately.
2. **Final consonant + Same beginning consonant**
   Pronounce one long consonant. Do not say the consonant twice.
3. **Final /st/ + Different beginning consonant**
   Final /st/ is often simplified to /s/ in common words when the next word begins with a consonant. This makes the phrase easier to say.

**C** ▶05-05 Listen. Complete the dialog. Then listen and repeat.

A: Oh, no! My laptop just shut down. And my report is only _____ .

B: I'll call tech support. They have a(n) _____ there.

A: This isn't the first time. It happened twice _____ .

B: Don't worry. If he _____ it, you can use mine.

# 4 CONVERSATION

**A** ▶05-06 Listen or watch. What do Michael and Pablo mainly talk about?

**B** ▶05-07 Listen or watch again. Answer the questions.

1. Why is Michael giving a presentation?
2. What four problems does Michael have with his laptop?
3. What does Pablo first suggest trying as a solution?
4. Who does Pablo go to get for help?

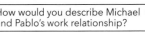
How would you describe Michael and Pablo's work relationship?

**C** ▶05-08 FOCUS ON LANGUAGE Listen or watch. Complete the conversation.

**Michael:** Hmm…that's strange. I thought I had this all set up and now I'm getting a(n) _____ .

**Pablo:** Error message? That's not good. Was it working OK earlier?

**Michael:** Yeah, there were no problems. I'd _____ at my presentation and everything seemed fine, and now the screen is _____ .

**Pablo:** Hmm…the same thing happened to me a few weeks ago.

# 5 TRY IT YOURSELF

**A** THINK When did you last have a technology problem? What was the problem? What had you been doing when the problem happened? Take notes.

**B** PAIRS Student A: Describe the technology problem you had. Use the information in 5A. Student B: Ask questions to get more information. Use the conversation in 4C as an example.

**C** REPORT Present your technology problems to the class. Which is the most common problem experienced by your classmates?

☐ I CAN DESCRIBE TECHNOLOGY PROBLEMS.

# LESSON 2  TALK ABOUT TECHNOLOGY SOLUTIONS

**MICHAEL STEWART**
@MichaelS

Ugh. Technology. Is it me or does it always go wrong at the worst time? Sometimes I think we'd be better off without it.

 **1 VOCABULARY** Technology solutions

**A** ▶05-09 **Listen. Then listen and repeat.**

> **reset:** to change something like a password or control so that it is ready to use again
> **recharge:** to put a new supply of electricity into a battery
> **reboot:** to start a computer after it has stopped working
> **install:** to add software to a computer so it is ready to use
> **restore:** to return a control setting to its original state
> **replace:** to get something new to put in place of something old or broken
> **reconnect:** to establish a connection to something like a server again
> **uninstall:** to remove a software program from a computer

**B** Label the pictures with words from 1A.

1. _____
a setting

3. _____
a device

5. _____
a program

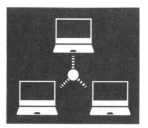

7. _____
to a network

2. _____
a battery

4. _____
antivirus software

6. _____
a power cord

8. _____
a password

**C** PAIRS Compare answers.

## 2 GRAMMAR  *Need* with gerunds and passive infinitives

*Need* can be followed by a gerund or a passive infinitive. The meaning is the same in both cases.

| *Need* + gerund | | | *Need* + passive infinitive | | |
|---|---|---|---|---|---|
| **Subject** | *Need* | **Gerund** | **Subject** | *Need* | **Passive infinitive** |
| The battery | needs | charging. | The battery | needs | to be charged. |
| Our employees | need | training. | Our employees | need | to be trained. |

>> FOR PRACTICE, GO TO PAGE 138

# 3 CONVERSATION SKILL

**A** ▶05-10 Read the conversation skill. Listen. Notice how Speaker B reassures Speaker A.

> **Reassure someone**
>
> When someone has a problem or is feeling worried, you can use expressions like these to help them feel better:
>
> *Don't worry.*                          *It's not a big deal.*
> *It's nothing to stress over.*    *This shouldn't be a problem.*
> *I've seen worse.*                     *Not a problem!*

1. A: My computer screen has frozen, and I haven't saved my files. I may have lost everything.
   B: It shouldn't be a problem. We can recover your files.
2. A: I think my computer might have a virus.
   B: Don't worry. I can get rid of it for you.

**B** PAIRS Practice the conversations.

# 4 CONVERSATION

**A** ▶05-11 Listen or watch. What problems does Michael report to Amy?

**B** ▶05-12 Listen or watch again. Answer the questions.

1. How does Michael feel when he sees Amy?
2. Why doesn't Amy think that the computer has a virus?
3. What is the last step Amy recommends to Michael?
4. How does Michael feel when Amy leaves? Why?

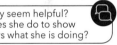
Does Amy seem helpful? What does she do to show she knows what she is doing?

**C** ▶05-13 FOCUS ON LANGUAGE Listen or watch. Complete the conversation.

> Michael: I restarted my computer, and everything looked fine, but now my presentation won't load. What do you think is wrong?
>
> Amy: Hmm...Let me take a look.
>
> Michael: Sure.
>
> Amy: Well, _____ a big deal. Some of your settings just _____ to be _____ . It'll only take a few minutes.

# 5 TRY IT YOURSELF

**A** THINK Imagine you have a technology problem with your phone. What is the best solution for it? Complete the chart.

| Problem | Solution |
|---------|----------|
|         |          |
|         |          |
|         |          |

**B** ROLE PLAY Student A: Report your technology problem to Student B. Student B: Tell Student A what needs to be done. Make sure you reassure Student A first. Use the conversation in 4C as an example.

**C** REPORT Tell the class about your partner's problem and solution. Does anyone else have any advice?

■ I CAN TALK ABOUT TECHNOLOGY SOLUTIONS.

### MICHAEL STEWART
@MichaelS

Watched this talk about technology making us lazier. Interesting, but I'm not sure I agree.

## 1 BEFORE YOU LISTEN

**A** What kinds of technology do you use that make your life easier? How often do you use them?

**B** ▶05-14 VOCABULARY Listen. Then listen and repeat.

> **depict:** to show someone or something using language or pictures
>
> **entertain:** to do something that interests people
>
> **exaggerate:** to make something seem bigger, better, or worse than it really is
>
> **a digital assistant:** a device that understands spoken language and allows you to control networked items in your home
>
> **a remote / a remote control:** a thing you use to control a device, such as a television
>
> **convenience:** the quality of being good or useful because it makes things easier
>
> **retain:** to keep information in your memory, such as numbers, dates, or facts
>
> **critical thinking:** the ability to make a careful judgment about something
>
> **media:** the organizations that provide news and information

**C** Complete the sentences with words from 1B.

1. I can tell my _____ to play music, change the TV channel, and turn on the lights.
2. I'm glad I can use my phone to remember all of the information I can't _____ .
3. Nowadays if you're bored, you always have the internet to _____ you.
4. I have one _____ for my TV and another for the audio. It's very annoying!
5. In the old days, there were a few TV channels and a lot of newspapers, but now the most important _____ source is the internet.
6. Getting food delivered is expensive, but you're paying for the _____ .
7. The new movie will _____ the life of a famous politician.
8. Paying attention to both sides of an argument can help you improve your _____ .
9. Companies often _____ the importance of their new technology. It's not usually very different from what we already have.

## 2 GRAMMAR Infinitives as subject complements

We sometimes use infinitives after the verb *be* to describe or identify a subject. These sentences often introduce a goal, purpose, or plan.

| Subject | *Be* | Infinitive | |
|---|---|---|---|
| Our goal | is | to move | as little as possible. |
| The purpose of technology | has been | to make | life easier. |
| Their plan | was | to develop | a safer car. |

**Note:** *Be* + infinitive usually appears after an **abstract noun**:
*His **advice** was to...*    *My **dream** is to...*    *Their **intention** was to...*    *The **effect** will be to...*

>> FOR PRACTICE, GO TO PAGE 139

# 3 LISTENING

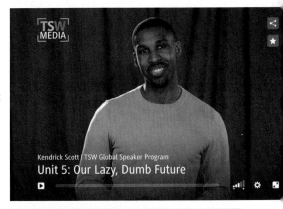

Kendrick Scott / TSW Global Speaker Program
**Unit 5: Our Lazy, Dumb Future**

**A** ▶05-15 Listen or watch. What is the speaker's intention?
   a. to explain how we need to improve technology
   b. to warn that technology could have a negative effect
   c. to convince us to stop using technology

**B** ▶05-16 Read the Listening Skill. Listen or watch again. Check (✓) the ideas that are introduced as counterarguments.

   ☐ a. The vision of the future in *Wall-E* is wildly exaggerated.
   ☐ b. Some people no longer leave the house to buy things.
   ☐ c. Digital assistants are a wonderful convenience.
   ☐ d. It's easy to ignore other people's opinions.
   ☐ e. I'm being unreasonable about technology. It makes life better.

> **LISTENING SKILL**
> **Listen for counterarguments**
>
> Speakers often present counterarguments–ideas they don't agree with–before they explain their own opinions. They may introduce counterarguments with expressions like:
> *You may think…*
> *Some people say…*
> *Many people believe…*

**C** ▶05-17 Listen or watch again. According to the speaker, which things could be making us lazier and / or less intelligent? Circle the items.

   a. shopping online      d. digital assistants       g. hundreds of TV channels
   b. movies               e. self-driving cars        h. washing machines
   c. social media         f. internet-connected refrigerators

**D** VOCABULARY EXPANSION  Read each sentence from the talk. What do the underlined expressions mean?

   1. You may think this vision of the future is wildly exaggerated, but I've got bad news for you, folks. I think we're <u>well on the way</u> there.

   _____

   2. <u>Brick-and-mortar stores</u> are closing all over the world as more and more of us decide not to leave the house to buy things.

   _____

   3. If a TV newsperson or a writer or my uncle on social media presents ideas that I don't like, I can just <u>tune them out</u> by changing the channel, or putting the book down, or clicking "unfollow."

   _____

**E** PAIRS  Compare answers in 3D.

# 4 DISCUSSION

**A** THINK  List three examples of modern technology not mentioned in the talk. What is the purpose of each one? How does it affect people? Take notes.

**B** DISCUSS  In small groups, share your examples and opinions from 4A.

**C** ANALYZE  Report to the class. Do you agree with what the speaker says about technology? What can we do, if anything, to prevent ourselves from becoming lazier and less intelligent?

☐ I CAN DISCUSS HOW TECHNOLOGY AFFECTS US.

# LESSON 4 READ AN ARTICLE ABOUT HACKING

MICHAEL STEWART
@MichaelS

I just read an article that made me rethink how I feel about hacking. Is it always such a terrible thing?

## 1 BEFORE YOU READ

**A** PAIRS Has anyone you know ever been hacked? What happened?

**B** ▶05-18 VOCABULARY Listen. Then listen and repeat. Do you know these words?

| justified | expose | corruption | confidential | outweigh |
| privacy | jeopardize | | | |

>> FOR DEFINITIONS AND PRACTICE, GO TO PAGE 139

## 2 READ

**A** PREVIEW Read the title and the subheadings. Look at the photos. What do you think the article will be about?

**B** ▶05-19 Read and listen to the article. Was your prediction correct?

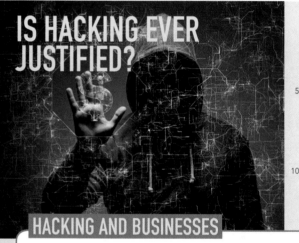

# IS HACKING EVER JUSTIFIED?

Hacking has become a big part of modern life. Every day, governments, organizations, businesses, and individuals are at risk of having their private information stolen and revealed. In fact, a University of Maryland study has shown
5 that one hacking attempt takes place about every 39 seconds. Everyone can probably agree that most kinds of hacking are wrong, such as stealing customers' financial data or removing photos from celebrities' phones. But what about when hacking reveals that something illegal has taken place? Or
10 when it exposes corruption? Are there any situations where hacking is actually justified?

## HACKING AND BUSINESSES

Take these cases for example. In recent years, major international law firms have been hacked. Information from the firms, which included millions
15 of personal documents, was passed on to journalists who published some of it on their news sites. Through these hacks, the public learned how some of the world's richest, most powerful people were spending and managing their money, in some cases
20 even to avoid paying taxes.

When this information was revealed, a lot of people were surprised and angry. They felt that the hacks were justified because they showed how the rich and powerful have access to systems that other
25 people don't. They strongly believed that the public had the right to know this kind of information. Not everyone, however, agreed that the ends justified the means. They thought that even the rich and powerful deserved to keep their information private.
30 They also worried that if it was OK to hack these people, what could protect other people?

## HACKING AND GOVERNMENTS

Other situations have involved individuals and organizations that have attempted to hack into governments, either their own or foreign ones.
35 Sometimes, these hackers manage to get sensitive information that they hand over to journalists or publish on their own websites for the whole world to see. This information often contains personal details about government officials and confidential documents about
40 government programs and operations.

People have very different opinions about this kind of hacking. On the one hand, some people believe that it is helpful to show what governments and government officials are doing. They claim that this enables citizens
45 to be more aware of their leaders' actions, in order to prevent things like corruption. On the other hand, critics say that these hackers go too far and are doing something potentially dangerous. They are concerned that this kind of hacking could reveal national secrets,
50 jeopardize people's careers, or even endanger their lives.

>>

In all these situations there are strong arguments for and against hacking and revealing private information to the public. Now that everyone is so connected to technology, cases like these are very likely to happen again. In the future, will people agree that
55 hacking can ever be justified? Will the public's right to know information ever outweigh individual privacy and national security? These questions remain to be answered, but everyone can agree on at least one thing: This debate about hacking is going to come up again.

## 3 CHECK YOUR UNDERSTANDING

**A** Read the article again. What is it about?

**B** Answer the questions, according to the article.

1. What kinds of hacking are usually considered wrong?

   _____

2. What did the public learn when major international law firms were hacked?

   _____

3. What did the public learn when governments were hacked?

   _____

4. Why is the hacking debate going to continue in the future?

   _____

**C** CLOSE READING Reread lines 6–10 in the article. Then circle the correct answers.

1. In line 6, the writer uses *probably* to show that ___ .
   a. it is possible that some people don't agree
   b. there are kinds of hacking that are not wrong
   c. most people usually like to agree with each other
2. The next two sentences are connected to the first sentence because they provide ___ .
   a. more examples of when hacking is definitely wrong
   b. examples of when hacking might be OK
   c. examples of things that hackers are not able to do

**D** Read the Reading Skill. Then reread the article. Underline the words and phrases that are used to show contrasts.

> **READING SKILL** Identify contrasts
>
> Writers often use specific words and phrases to signal contrasts. They include *but, however, although, on the one hand,* and *on the other hand.*

**E** PAIRS What is the article about? Retell the most important ideas. Use your own words.

> What is a recent case of hacking that caught the public's attention? 🔍

## 4 MAKE IT PERSONAL

**A** THINK Do you think hacking is ever justified? Give reasons for each opinion.

| Hacking is justified when: | Hacking isn't justified when: |
|---|---|
|  |  |
|  |  |

**B** PAIRS Share your ideas from 4A.

⬛ I CAN READ AN ARTICLE ABOUT HACKING.

### MICHAEL STEWART
@MichaelS

I just got a new camera that takes 360-degree videos and images. Check out the photo I took and read my review!

## 1 BEFORE YOU WRITE

**A** How do you decide to buy something new, especially something expensive like a camera?

**B** Complete the sentences with the words in the box.

| playback | upgrade | compact |
| --- | --- | --- |

1. Nina's new phone is definitely a(n) _____ from her old one. It has so many cool new features.
2. The _____ feature on the video camera lets us watch and listen to what we had just recorded right away.
3. This new phone has all the same features, but it is smaller and more _____ .

**C** Read the review. What is Michael's purpose in writing this review?

---

### Review: **The GV500 360-Degree Video Camera**

My greatest passions are ice hockey, windsurfing, and digital media. So I was really excited when the new GV500 360-degree camera came out. Not only does it have many new features, but the videos and pictures I shoot with it make me feel like I'm in the middle of the action again.

**BEST FEATURES**

First of all, the GV500 is the easiest to use of all the 360-degree cameras in its price range. It's light and compact, which is very important for me when I'm carrying other equipment. Its design is also really attractive, but it is sturdy enough for me to use in the middle of fast-paced sports action. And, when I am shooting windsurfers, it's good to know that the GV500 is waterproof to 12 meters, which is up from 4 meters for the GV400. In addition, some of the GV500's technical qualities are especially important for my digital design work. The audio quality is great and uploading to social media is very simple.

**ROOM FOR IMPROVEMENT**

However, there are still some ways the GV500 could be improved. For example, even though they've made using it as simple as possible, there is still a lot to learn. If you are not very technical, this could be a problem. I also found that the image quality is not as good as it could be. It's fine for posting things on social media, but when I do business presentations, the playback is not good enough on large computer or TV screens. Then there's the price. At about $200, I had to ask myself whether this new model was that much better than the old one.

**TO BUY, OR NOT TO BUY**

Obviously, my answer was "Yes," and I am very happy I bought it. If you are buying your first 360-degree camera, or want an upgrade from your current one, I recommend the GV500. As for some of its drawbacks, I hope they'll be solved when the GV600 comes out!

**D** Read the review again. Complete the chart with the pros and cons of the GV500.

| GV500 Pros | GV500 Cons |
|---|---|
|  |  |

## 2 FOCUS ON WRITING

Read the Writing Skill. Then reread the review. Underline the subheadings in the review. Which one introduces the pros, cons, and conclusion?

## 3 PLAN YOUR WRITING

**A** THINK What have you bought recently? Are there features you like about this product? Is there anything you don't like? Draw a chart like the one in 1D.

**B** PAIRS Talk about the product and its pros and cons.

## 4 WRITE

Write a review of a product you bought recently. Explain why you bought it, its pros and cons, and why you would or wouldn't recommend it to others. Use a subheading for each paragraph. Use the review in 1C as a model.

**Writing tip**

When you write a review of a product to post online, think about the interests of your readers. Some people won't have time to read your whole review, so keep your points clear and simple, and put the most important points first.

## 5 REVISE YOUR WRITING

**A** PAIRS Exchange product reviews and read each other's writing.
1. Did your partner clearly explain why he or she bought the product?
2. Did your partner include the pros and the cons of the product?
3. Did your partner include a relevant subheading for each paragraph?

**B** PAIRS Can your partner improve his or her product review? Make suggestions.

## 6 PROOFREAD

Read your product review again. Check your
- spelling
- punctuation
- capitalization

I CAN **WRITE A PRODUCT REVIEW.**

# PUT IT TOGETHER

## 1 PRESENTATION PROJECT

**A** ▶05-20 Listen or watch. What is the topic of the presentation?

**B** ▶05-21 Listen or watch again. Answer the questions.

1. Where are some companies putting solar panels?
   _____

2. What would the bottom layer of these new solar panels do?
   _____

3. What are the benefits of using solar panels on roads?
   _____

**C** Read the presentation skill. Have you ever tried to use this skill?

**D** Make your own presentation.

Step 1  Do research about an advance in technology. Describe the advance and its effects.

Step 2  Prepare a two-minute presentation about the advance in technology. Bring an item or photo related to the technology.

> **PRESENTATION SKILL**
>
> **Speak slowly and clearly**
> Be careful not to rush through your presentation. Pronounce words carefully and pause occasionally.

Step 3  Give your presentation to the class. Remember to use the presentation skill. Answer questions and get feedback.

How did you do? Complete the self-evaluation on page 165.

## 2 REFLECT AND PLAN

**A** Look back through the unit. Check (✓) the things you learned. Highlight the things you need to learn.

**Speaking objectives**
- ☐ Describe technology problems
- ☐ Talk about technology solutions
- ☐ Discuss how technology affects us

**Vocabulary**
- ☐ Technology problems
- ☐ Technology solutions

**Conversation**
- ☐ Reassure someone

**Pronunciation**
- ☐ Link final consonants to beginning consonants

**Listening**
- ☐ Listen for counterarguments

**Grammar**
- ☐ Past perfect continuous
- ☐ *Need* with gerunds and passive infinitives
- ☐ Infinitives as subject complements

**Reading**
- ☐ Identify contrasts

**Writing**
- ☐ Write relevant subheadings

**B** What will you do to learn the things you highlighted? For example, use your app, review your Student Book, or do other practice. Make a plan.

> ‹ Notes                    Done
>
> In the app, do the Lesson 1 Conversation activities: Describe technology problems
> _____
> _____
> _____

# 6 WHERE WAS IT MADE?

## LEARNING GOALS

In this unit, you
- ⊗ describe a decorative object
- ⊗ describe music you like
- ⊗ discuss traditional food
- ⊗ read an article supporting a point of view
- ⊗ write about how to do something

## GET STARTED

**A** Read the unit title and learning goals.

**B** Look at the photo. What's going on?

**C** Now read Hana's message. Where is she going? What does she have?

### HANA LEE
@HanaL

Headed back to New York to work on the new ad campaign. Brought lots of gifts for everyone!

**HANA LEE**
@HanaL

Just got to the office. Looking forward to catching up with some old friends and colleagues.

 ## 1 VOCABULARY
Materials and decorative objects

**A** ▶06-01 Listen. Then listen and repeat.

| | | | |
|---|---|---|---|
| a glass vase | a stone bowl | a silver picture frame | a ceramic figurine |
| a leather case | a rubber toy | a vinyl bag | a silk bookmark |

**B** Sort the materials in 1A into two categories. Then add other materials you know.

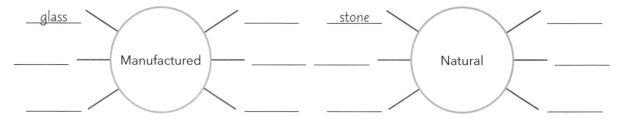

glass _____          stone _____

Manufactured          Natural

**C** PAIRS Think of five things you have that are made of the materials in 1B. Compare lists.
A: I have a stone figurine.
B: We both have a silver ring...

## 2 GRAMMAR Simple present and simple past passive: Review

Use the passive when it is not important or known who performs or performed an action.

| Questions | | | | | Statements | | | |
|---|---|---|---|---|---|---|---|---|
| | **Wh-word** | **Be** | **Subject** | **Past participle** | | **Subject** | **Be** | **Past participle** | |
| **Present** | What | is | it | made | of? | It | is | made | of wood. |
| | How | are | they | used? | | They | are | used | as pillows. |
| **Past** | Where | was | it | designed? | | It | was | designed | in Korea. |
| | When | were | they | built? | | They | were | built | in 1850. |

**Note:** Passive sentences sometimes include a *by* phrase that explains who did the action:
*It was made **by** a local artist.*

>> FOR PRACTICE, GO TO PAGE 140

# 3 CONVERSATION SKILL

**A** ▶06-02 Read the conversation skill. Listen. Notice how Speaker B replies with surprise by turning Speaker A's statements into a question.

> **Express surprise**
>
> You can express surprise by using rising intonation to turn a statement into a question.

1. A: Mike's car has leather seats.
   B: It has leather seats?

2. A: Kate and Sam are getting a glass table.
   B: They're getting a glass table?

**B** ▶06-03 Listen. Is the speaker making a statement or expressing surprise? Write a period (.) or a question mark (?).

1. ____    3. ____    5. ____
2. ____    4. ____    6. ____

# 4 CONVERSATION

**A** ▶06-04 Listen or watch. What do Oscar and Hana talk about?

**B** ▶06-05 Listen or watch again. Answer the questions.

1. Where did Hana fly in from?
2. What does Oscar say about a messy desk?
3. Why does Hana ask Oscar to clear a space on his desk?
4. What will Oscar do with the chopstick rest?

> Do you think Hana usually brings gifts for her co-workers? Why or why not?

**C** ▶06-06 FOCUS ON LANGUAGE Listen or watch. Complete the conversation.

> **Hana:** I brought you a small gift. All the way from Korea, not from LA!
>
> **Oscar:** Wow! Thanks! You shouldn't have! Beautiful. I love the color. But, um, what is it exactly?
>
> **Hana:** Oh! It's a traditional Korean chopstick rest.
>
> **Oscar:** _____? It's really beautiful, and I love the way it feels. What is it _____ of?
>
> **Hana:** It's a kind of _____ .
>
> **Oscar:** Cool!

# 5 TRY IT YOURSELF

**A** THINK Choose a decorative object you love. Complete the chart.

| What is it? | Where was it made? | What's it made of? | What's it used for? |
|---|---|---|---|
|  |  |  |  |

**B** PAIRS Student A: Describe the object in 5A. Student B: Ask questions to get more information about the object. Use the conversation in 4C as an example.

**C** REPORT Tell the class about your partner's object.

☐ I CAN DESCRIBE A DECORATIVE OBJECT.

# LESSON 2     DESCRIBE MUSIC YOU LIKE

**HANA LEE**

@HanaL

Someone once said that the world's most famous and popular language is music. I totally agree!

 ## 1 VOCABULARY
Musical terms and descriptions

**A** ▶06-07 **Listen. Then listen and repeat.**

---

**Musical terms**

**beat:** the main pattern of sounds in a song

**melody:** a tune in a song

**lyrics:** the words of a song

**vocals:** the part of a song that is sung

**Ways to describe music**

**cheerful:** bright, pleasant, and making you feel happy

**catchy:** easy to remember and nice to listen to

**mellow:** relaxed and calm

**lively:** active, energetic, fast-paced

**clever:** done in an unusual or interesting way

**powerful:** having a strong effect on your feelings

**funky:** having a strong bass beat; easy to dance to

---

**B** ▶06-08 **Listen. Write the number of the conversation that matches each sentence.**

a. It has a lively beat. _____

b. It has a catchy melody. _____

c. It has clever lyrics. _____

d. It has powerful vocals. _____

**C** PAIRS Choose one song or singer for each category. Then compare answers. Do you agree with your partner's choices?

| Catchy melody | Powerful vocals | Clever lyrics | Lively beat |
| --- | --- | --- | --- |
| _____ | _____ | _____ | _____ |

## 2 GRAMMAR Restrictive and non-restrictive relative clauses: Review and expand

Use restrictive relative clauses to add essential information about the subject or object of the main clause. Use non-restrictive relative clauses to add extra but non-essential information. Use a relative pronoun or relative adverb to introduce a relative clause.

| Main clause | Restrictive relative clause | |
| --- | --- | --- |
| It's different from the music | (that) I've been listening to. | |

| Main Clause | Non-restrictive relative clause | |
| --- | --- | --- |
| It's her latest song, | which she released last week. | |
| My best friend, | who's in a local band, | got me interested in it. |

Relative pronouns and relative adverbs introduce relative clauses.

**Relative pronouns**
who, that, which, whom, whose

**Relative adverbs**
where, when, whenever, wherever

**Notes**

• Non-restrictive relative clauses cannot begin with *that*.

• Use commas with non-restrictive clauses but not with restrictive clauses.

# 3 PRONUNCIATION

**A** ▶06-09 Read and listen to the pronunciation note.

**B** ▶06-10 Listen. Notice the pausing. Notice the low intonation with the non-restrictive relative clauses. Then listen and repeat.

1. Colombian music, /which has a lively beat,/ is great for dancing.
2. The lyrics, /which tell a story of lost love,/ are so sad.
3. David Bowie wrote the song that you just played.
4. The singer that won the contest/ was only 15.

**C** ▶06-11 Listen. Mark the pauses you hear with a slash (/) and underline the clauses where the intonation drops. Add commas (,) to the non-restrictive relative clauses.

1. The guitar that I usually play is really old, but it has a sound that I love.
2. This guitar which was given to me by my mother used to belong to my grandfather.

> **Pausing and intonation with relative clauses**
>
> <u>Restrictive relative clauses</u>
> There is usually no pause before a restrictive relative clause. There may be a pause after a restrictive relative clause when it occurs in the middle of a sentence.
>
> <u>Non-restrictive relative clauses</u>
> We pause before and after a non-restrictive relative clause. Intonation is lower over the clause.

# 4 CONVERSATION

**A** ▶06-12 Listen or watch. What do Oscar and Hana talk about?

**B** ▶06-13 Listen or watch again. Answer the questions.

1. What kind of music is Hana listening to?
2. Why does she like it?
3. What does Hana think of Oscar's music?
4. What will Oscar send Hana later?

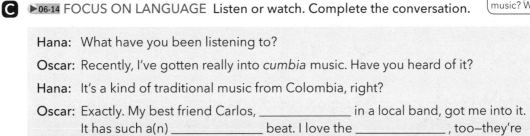

> Do you think Oscar and Hana will continue listening to each other's music? Why or why not?

**C** ▶06-14 FOCUS ON LANGUAGE Listen or watch. Complete the conversation.

| | |
|---|---|
| **Hana:** | What have you been listening to? |
| **Oscar:** | Recently, I've gotten really into *cumbia* music. Have you heard of it? |
| **Hana:** | It's a kind of traditional music from Colombia, right? |
| **Oscar:** | Exactly. My best friend Carlos, _____ in a local band, got me into it. It has such a(n) _____ beat. I love the _____ , too–they're so catchy. |
| **Hana:** | Great! |

# 5 TRY IT YOURSELF

**A** THINK What types of music do you like? Why do you like them? Take notes.

**B** PAIRS Compare answers. Do you like the same types of music? Why or why not? Use the conversation in 4C as an example.

**C** TAKE A POLL Which types of music are the most popular in the class? Which are the least popular?

■ I CAN DESCRIBE MUSIC I LIKE.

# LESSON 3    DISCUSS TRADITIONAL FOOD

**HANA LEE**
@HanaL

Love international food? Your favorite dishes might not be as authentic as you think. You've gotta watch this video.

## 1 BEFORE YOU LISTEN

**A** How often do you eat out in a restaurant? What kinds of food do you like to order?

**B** ▶06-15 VOCABULARY  Listen. Then listen and repeat.

> **admit:** to say that you have done something wrong, or that something bad is true
> **a dish:** food that you prepare in a particular way
> **authentic:** to really be what people say it is, not fake
> **tolerate:** to endure an experience, without it having a bad effect on your body
> **appeal to:** to seem attractive or interesting to someone
> **a version:** a form of something that is slightly different from other forms
> **an ingredient:** one of the things that you use to make a particular food
> **an immigrant:** someone who enters another country to live there

**C** Complete the sentences with words from 1B.

1. A Japanese _____ started this restaurant. These dishes taste just like the food I had in Japan.
2. I _____ that I eat too much fast food–I'm just too busy to cook these days!
3. This Chinese restaurant isn't very _____ ; few items on the menu would ever be served in China.
4. I cook a(n) _____ of this sweet and sour pork _____ at home, but I use less sugar.
5. In Korea, pizza is often served with toppings like corn to _____ local tastes.
6. Red chili pepper is a(n) _____ that is added to food to make it spicier.
7. My niece can't _____ cow's milk. She has to drink goat's milk and eat goat's cheese.

## 2 GRAMMAR  *You, they, can / can't, could / couldn't for general truths*

> We sometimes use *can / can't* to talk about something that is generally true in the present and *could / couldn't* to talk about something that is generally true in the past. In both cases, we can use *you* or *they* as the subjects.
>
> In large cities, **you can** get cuisine from all different parts of the world.
>
> **They can't** serve horse meat in restaurants in the US.
>
> In years past, you **could** rarely find fresh fruit in winter.
>
> Not so long ago, **you couldn't** get real Thai food ingredients outside of Thailand.
>
> Notes
> - Use *you* for people in general.
> - Use *they* for people in authority, such as business owners, people in government, and people in charge of organizations.

**>> FOR PRACTICE, GO TO PAGE 142**

# 3 LISTENING

 **A** ▶06-16 Listen or watch. What is the main idea of the talk?

 **B** ▶06-17 Read the Listening Skill. Listen or watch again. Match each example with the idea it supports in the talk.

David Cruz | TSW Global Speaker Program
**Unit 6: Traditional Food—Not!**

> **LISTENING SKILL** Listen for supporting details
>
> Supporting details make the main idea stronger. A supporting detail can be an example or a reason. To identify supporting details, listen for words and phrases like *for example, one reason,* and *This is why.*

___ 1. Italian food
___ 2. deep-dish pizza
___ 3. Indian vindaloo curry
___ 4. canned food

a. a way to get authentic ingredients
b. an authentically spicy dish
c. global cuisine you can find in most cities
d. a food that is not really traditional

 **C** ▶06-18 Listen or watch again. Which two reasons does the speaker give for why traditional food is not always authentic in different countries?

a. Traditional food is too expensive.
b. Dishes are changed to match people's tastes.
c. Ingredients are not always available.

**D** VOCABULARY EXPANSION Read each sentence from the talk. What do the underlined expressions mean?

1. One reason that food gets <u>lost in translation</u> when introduced to a new culture is that the locals may not be used to, or ready for, certain foreign tastes.

   _____

2. There's another reason that traditional dishes are not always so traditional, and that <u>has to do with</u> ingredients.

   _____

3. <u>The bottom line is this</u>: The fish tacos you get in your local Mexican restaurant probably won't taste quite like the ones you'd have in Mexico, but you can enjoy them all the same!

   _____

**E** PAIRS Compare answers in 3D.

# 4 DISCUSSION

**A** THINK What new restaurant would you like to see open in your neighborhood? Should it serve authentic dishes or create new versions adapted to local tastes? Write three reasons to support your opinion.

**B** DISCUSS In small groups, share your opinions and reasons from 4A.

**C** EVALUATE As a class, choose the best three reasons for each opinion and write them on the board. Then vote on whether the restaurant should feature authentic or adapted dishes.

■ I CAN DISCUSS TRADITIONAL FOOD.

# READ AN ARTICLE SUPPORTING A POINT OF VIEW

**HANA LEE**
@HanaL

What do you think of men wearing skirts? It's actually not as unusual as it seems.

## 1 BEFORE YOU READ

**A** PAIRS Have you ever seen someone wearing something you thought was unusual? What was it?

**B** ▶06-19 VOCABULARY Listen. Then listen and repeat. Do you know these words?

> a dress code  prohibit  a loophole  a controversy  a garment  a trend  the norm
> **>> FOR DEFINITIONS AND PRACTICE, GO TO PAGE 142**

## 2 READ

**A** PREVIEW Read the title and look at the pictures. What do you think the article will be about?

**B** ▶06-20 Read and listen to the article. Was your prediction correct?

# THE RIGHT TO CHOOSE COMFORT

One particularly hot summer in Europe, some male bus drivers in France and schoolboys in England were faced with a similar problem. They wanted to stay cool, but the dress codes where they worked and studied prohibited them from wearing shorts. After thinking about the problem for a while, they came up with a solution.
5 They realized that there was a loophole in their dress codes, and they started wearing skirts instead of long pants.

Although some people thought that their idea was funny and clever, not everyone was impressed. For other people, it was unusual, even shocking, for men and boys to wear skirts in public places. But why should this create such a controversy? There
10 are actually plenty of reasons why men and boys should feel free to wear skirts.

To begin with, men have been wearing skirt-like garments in Western countries for thousands of years. In Ancient Greece and Rome, for example, male soldiers used to wear a piece of cloth that looked like a skirt. And of course, kilts have always been acceptable for men to wear in Scotland. It is also common for people in many
15 other parts of the world to still wear clothing that resembles skirts. In Thailand, for instance, men sometimes wrap a long, skirt-like piece of material around their legs while working, relaxing, and traveling. Moreover, skirts are a lot more comfortable than many other types of clothing, especially in hot weather and tropical locations. Many of them are made from light materials that help their wearers to stay cool. In addition, skirts can
20 be very attractive and fashionable. They come in a wide variety of colors and designs that help people look good and stand out.

Over the last few decades, some famous Western fashion designers and celebrities have been seen promoting and wearing skirts for men. In 1984, the legendary French fashion designer Jean Paul Gaultier made history by showing off men in skirts at a fashion show in Paris.
25 Nowadays, skirts for men are available from many different clothing companies and online shopping websites. As for celebrities, American actor Vin Diesel and British soccer sensation David Beckham have been photographed wearing skirts in public places.

>>

> Does this mean that we should expect to see more men and boys wearing skirts in public places in the future? That remains to be
30 determined. The actions of the British schoolboys and French bus drivers did not launch a new global fashion trend. However, they did raise awareness of the issue and got more people thinking positively about the possibility of men wearing skirts. So, men in skirts might not become the norm in the coming years, but the idea does slowly seem to be gaining
35 acceptance. At the very least, men and boys now have another option when the weather gets too hot for them to wear long pants.

## 3 CHECK YOUR UNDERSTANDING

**A** Read the article again. What is the main idea?

**B** Answer the questions, according to the article.

1. Why were the men and boys not allowed to wear shorts to work or school?
   _____

2. How did the men and boys solve this problem?
   _____

3. How did people feel about the solution that the men and boys came up with?
   _____

4. Does the writer think that more men and boys will wear skirts in the future?
   _____

**C** CLOSE READING Reread lines 17-19 in the article. Then circle the correct answers.

1. In line 19, the word *them* refers to ___ .
   a. other types of clothing
   b. tropical locations
   c. skirts
2. In line 19, the writer mentions light materials to give a reason why ___ .
   a. skirts are more comfortable than other types of clothes
   b. other types of clothes are more comfortable than skirts
   c. skirts are not good for some people in tropical locations

**D** Read the Reading Skill. Then reread the article.

1. Underline the phrase that introduces the argument about wearing skirts.
2. Circle the words or phrases that add more reasons.

**E** PAIRS What is the article about? Retell the most important ideas. Use your own words.

> **READING SKILL** Identify supporting reasons
>
> Writers often provide reasons to support their arguments. Sometimes they introduce the reasons with expressions such as *there are several reasons why*. Then they add more reasons with words and phrases like *to begin with, also, in addition, what's more,* and *furthermore*.

> What is a new fashion trend where you live?

## 4 MAKE IT PERSONAL

**A** THINK Remember a time when you thought a dress code or another rule wasn't fair. Why did you think the dress code or rule was unfair? What did you do?

**B** PAIRS Share your experiences. How did your classmates feel about the rules they thought were unfair? What did they do?

☐ I CAN READ AN ARTICLE SUPPORTING A POINT OF VIEW.

# LESSON 5 · WRITE ABOUT HOW TO DO SOMETHING

## HANA LEE
@HanaL

Did you know that there's a right way to eat pizza in New York? Read my new blog post to find out!

## 1 BEFORE YOU WRITE

**A** How do you usually eat pizza? Do you ever use a knife and fork?

**B** Read Hana's blog. What did she recently learn how to do?

---

Blog  About  Contact                                    🔍 Search

# Eating Pizza Like a New Yorker

About
RSS Feed
Social Media
Recent Posts
Archives
Email

Every time I'm at the New York City office, I like to try something new for lunch. Yesterday, I checked out a famous pizza place with some co-workers and learned the secret of eating pizza like a New Yorker. Here's what I found out.

To begin with, you have to choose what kind of pizza you want right away. Most pizza places in New York City sell pizza by the slice. They keep their pizza inside a glass case near the front door. So, you have to step up to the case and tell the clerk what kind of pizza you want and how many slices you need. Sometimes, you have to wait for the clerk to warm them up. Once your slices are ready, you can take them to an empty table and sit down.

Next, you need to decide if you want to add any of the extra toppings at the table to your pizza. A lot of pizza places provide red pepper flakes, parmesan cheese, and black pepper. I like to add a little parmesan cheese to my slices. This makes them taste even cheesier!

After that, you have to figure out how to hold each slice so you can eat it. There are a couple of different ways to do this. For example, you can simply fold it in half from one side of the crust to the other. You can also bend it in half by pushing down on the middle of the crust with one finger. Then you can put your other fingers underneath to support it. Just never, ever, cut it with a knife and fork!

Last but not least, make sure you enjoy what you're eating. New Yorkers put a lot of effort into making great pizza, and they're really proud of their work. So, the least you can do is show that you loved every bite.

As you can see, it's really not that hard to eat pizza like a New Yorker. It just takes a little practice. Now that I know how, I can't wait to go back and try out some of the other famous pizza places in the city.

**Leave a Reply**

Enter your comment here...

**C** Read the blog again. Take notes in the chart.

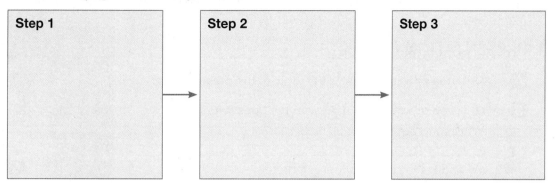

| Step 1 | Step 2 | Step 3 |
|--------|--------|--------|
|        |        |        |

## 2 FOCUS ON WRITING

Read the Writing Skill. Then reread Hana's blog. Underline the words and phrases she uses to show the sequence of events.

## 3 PLAN YOUR WRITING

**A** THINK What is something that you have recently learned how to do? What are the steps in the process? Draw a chart like the one in 1C.

**B** PAIRS Explain the process.

I recently learned a great new way to make guacamole. To begin with, you need to go out and find some really fresh avocados...

## 4 WRITE

Write a blog about something that you have recently learned how to do. Be sure to include at least three steps. Remember to use words and phrases to show the sequence of events. Use the blog in 1B as a model.

**Pre-writing tip**
Make a mental image of each step in the process. This will help you to explain the steps clearly and completely.

## 5 REVISE YOUR WRITING

**A** PAIRS Exchange blogs and read each other's writing.
1. Did your partner include at least three steps? Underline them.
2. Did your partner use words and phrases to show the sequence of events? Circle them.

**B** PAIRS Can your partner improve his or her blog? Make suggestions.

## 6 PROOFREAD

Read your blog again. Check your
- spelling
- punctuation
- capitalization

☐ I CAN WRITE ABOUT HOW TO DO SOMETHING.

# PUT IT TOGETHER

## 1 PRESENTATION PROJECT

**A** ▶06-21 Listen or watch. What is the topic of the presentation?

**B** ▶06-22 Listen or watch again. Answer the questions.

1. What culture is the *quinceañera* from?
   _____

2. What does the *quinceañera* celebrate?
   _____

3. What three customs does the *quinceañera* include?
   _____

**C** Read the presentation skill. How can you remember to use this skill?

**D** Make your own presentation.

**Step 1** Research a tradition from a culture that you're familiar with.

**Step 2** Prepare a two-minute presentation about the tradition. Include what the tradition is, what culture it is from, what customs it includes, and why it interests you. Bring an item or picture that is related to the tradition.

**Step 3** Give your presentation to the class. Remember to use the presentation skill. Answer questions and get feedback.

> ### PRESENTATION SKILL
> **Vary your intonation**
> As you are speaking, make your voice rise and fall instead of speaking in a monotone. This will make your voice easier to understand and more interesting.

How did you do? Complete the self-evaluation on page 165.

## 2 REFLECT AND PLAN

**A** Look back through the unit. Check (✓) the things you learned. Highlight the things you need to learn.

**Speaking objectives**
- ☐ Describe a decorative object
- ☐ Describe music you like
- ☐ Discuss traditional food

**Vocabulary**
- ☐ Materials and decorative objects
- ☐ Musical terms and descriptions

**Conversation**
- ☐ Express surprise

**Pronunciation**
- ☐ Pausing and intonation with relative clauses

**Listening**
- ☐ Listen for supporting details

**Grammar**
- ☐ Simple present and simple past passive
- ☐ Restrictive and non-restrictive relative clauses
- ☐ *You, they, can / can't, could / couldn't* for general truths

**Reading**
- ☐ Identify supporting reasons

**Writing**
- ☐ Show the sequence of events

**B** What will you do to learn the things you highlighted? For example, use your app, review your Student Book, or do other practice. Make a plan.

> ‹ Notes          Done
>
> Review the Listening Skill: Listen for supporting details, page 71.
> _____
> _____
> _____
> _____

# 7 WHEN DO YOU FLY OUT?

## LEARNING GOALS

In this unit, you

- ⊘ talk about air travel preferences
- ⊘ talk about travel memories
- ⊘ discuss past transportation predictions
- ⊘ read about unique transportation systems
- ⊘ write a thank-you email

## GET STARTED

**A** Read the unit title and learning goals.

**B** Look at the photo. What's going on?

**C** Now read Elena's message. How does she feel about traveling?

### ELENA RUBIO
@ElenaR

I always say the best part of traveling is what happens on the way there. What do you think?

**ELENA RUBIO**
@ElenaR

There are aisle-seat people and window-seat people. No one is a middle-seat person, right?

## 1 VOCABULARY  Air travel terms

**A** ▶07-01 **Listen. Then listen and repeat.**

> **landing:** the act of bringing a plane down to the ground
> **takeoff:** the act of making a plane rise into the air
> **a terminal:** a building where people wait to get on planes
> **a carry-on:** a small bag that a person is allowed to take on a plane
> **a boarding pass:** an official document that a person has to show before getting on a plane
> **security:** the area of an airport where people and their bags are checked for illegal items
> **an aisle:** a long passage between rows of seats on a plane
> **economy class:** the cheapest type of seats on a plane
> **business class:** seats on a plane that are more expensive than economy class
> **first class:** the most expensive seats on a plane

**B** Complete the sentences with words from 1A.

1. I love flying business class, but usually I can only afford to fly _____ .
2. While _____ , the buildings below us started to look bigger and bigger.
3. You must show your ID and _____ before you can get on the plane.
4. Your carry-on is checked by an X-ray machine at _____ .
5. _____ is located between first class and economy class.
6. Just before _____ , we watched a short safety video on the plane.
7. Our flight is leaving from gate 18 in _____ 2.
8. You should take only one _____ with you on the plane.
9. _____ is the most expensive, but it also has the most space.
10. Last time I got a window seat, but this time I got a(n) _____ seat.

**C** PAIRS  Talk about the last time you flew. Use the words from 1A.

## 2 GRAMMAR  Comparisons with gerund and noun phrases

Use gerund and noun phrases to make comparisons between ideas or things. We can use them to talk about preferences and the advantages and disadvantages of something.

| Statements | | | | | |
| --- | --- | --- | --- | --- | --- |
| **Noun phrase** | **Verb** | **(Not)** | **Comparative** | **Than** | **Noun phrase** |
| That terminal | is | (not) | less / more crowded | than | the other terminals. |
| **Gerund phrase** | | | | | **Gerund phrase** |
| Sitting on the aisle | is | (not) | better / worse | than | sitting next to the window. |

| Questions | | | | |
| --- | --- | --- | --- | --- |
| **Verb** | **Noun phrase** | **Comparative** | **Than** | **Noun phrase** |
| Is | that terminal | less / more crowded | than | the other terminals? |
| | **Gerund phrase** | | | **Gerund phrase** |
| Is | sitting on the aisle | better / worse | than | sitting next to the window? |

>> FOR PRACTICE, GO TO PAGE 143

# 3 PRONUNCIATION

**A** ▶07-02 Read and listen to the pronunciation note.

**Reduced pronunciation of *than***

The comparative conjunction *than* is unstressed, and the vowel is reduced to /ə/: /ðən/.
*Than* is very short and blends with the words around it. The comparative words *more* and *less* are both stressed.

**B** ▶07-03 Listen. Notice how *than* is reduced. Then listen again and repeat.

1. Terminal 5 is less crowded than other terminals.
2. The food on this flight was a lot better than the food on my last flight.
3. Overnight flights are often cheaper than daytime flights.

**C** PAIRS Practice the sentences in 3B. Create your own sentences using *than*.

# 4 CONVERSATION

**A** ▶07-04 Listen or watch. What do Elena and Gina talk about?

**B** ▶07-05 Listen or watch again. Answer the questions.

1. What is Elena doing when Gina greets her?
2. What kind of seat did Elena get on the plane?
3. What does Elena need to do before she forgets?
4. Why doesn't Elena like to use the airline app?

Do you think Elena will use an airline app the next time she flies? Would you use one?

**C** ▶07-06 FOCUS ON LANGUAGE Listen or watch. Complete the conversation.

> **Gina:** You like sitting next to the window? I prefer an _____ seat myself.
>
> **Elena:** Really?
>
> **Gina:** Yeah. It's _____ sitting next to the window. It's so much easier to get up and move around.
>
> **Elena:** True. But don't you hate having to get up for people when they want to get in or out? That always bothers me.

# 5 TRY IT YOURSELF

**A** THINK What are your air travel preferences? Think about things like making reservations, checking in, and seating. Use the adjectives in the box and your own ideas.

| faster / slower | more convenient / inconvenient | more comfortable / uncomfortable |
| --- | --- | --- |
| safer / more dangerous | more relaxing / stressful | easier / more difficult |

**B** PAIRS Compare your preferences. Use the conversation in 4C as an example.

A: I find checking my bags more convenient than walking around the terminal with them.
B: Really? I prefer taking my bags on the plane with me.

**C** REPORT Tell the class about your travel preferences. What are the most common air travel preferences? Do most people have the same preferences?

■ I CAN TALK ABOUT AIR TRAVEL PREFERENCES.

**ELENA RUBIO**
@ElenaR

What's the safest form of transportation? Surprise! It's the airplane, followed by the bus, subway, train, ferry, car, and motorcycle.

## 1 VOCABULARY
Train and car travel terms

**A** ▶07-07 Listen. Then listen and repeat.

> **Train travel terms**
> **the tracks:** two metal lines along which trains travel
> **a delay:** a situation in which someone or something is made to wait
> **on time:** at the right time, and not early or late
> **a car:** one of the connected parts of a train that people sit in
> **on board:** on a train, ship, or plane
> **Car travel terms**
> **a road trip:** a long journey you take in a car, usually with friends
> **a breakdown:** when a car stops working during a trip and must be fixed
> **a roof rack:** a frame attached to the top of a car that allows you to store things
> **a trunk:** the part at the back of a car where you can put bags and other large things
> **the brakes:** the equipment that makes a car slow down or stop

**B** ▶07-08 Listen. Which travel term is the speaker describing? Write a word or phrase from 1A.

1. _____   4. _____   7. _____   9. _____
2. _____   5. _____   8. _____   10. _____
3. _____   6. _____

**C** PAIRS What are the differences between train travel and a road trip?

## 2 GRAMMAR Past habits with *would* / *used to*: Review and expand

We can use *would* and *used to* to talk about habits that don't happen anymore.

|  | Subject | *Would / used to* | Base form of the verb |  |
|---|---|---|---|---|
| When I was a child, | I | would / used to | travel | by train. |
| As a child, | you | didn't use to | | |

**Notes**
- When we talk about the past, *would* often has the same meaning as *used to*. However, *would* can only be used for past habits, while *used to* can be used for past habits, states, and situations. The simple past can also be used for past states and situations: *Sam used to be a pilot. / Sam was a pilot.* NOT: ~~Sam would be a pilot.~~
- When we talk about past habits, it is clearer to start by using *used to* rather than *would* so the listener is sure we're talking about the past.
- Use *use to* instead of *used to* for questions and negative statements with *did*: *Did…use to…?* or *I didn't use to…*
- We often use *would* instead of *used to* or the simple past when talking about happy memories.
- Use the simple past to talk about past events that happened only once.

>> FOR PRACTICE, GO TO PAGE 144

# 3 CONVERSATION SKILL

Ⓐ ▶07-09 Read the conversation skill. Listen. Notice that Speaker B responds by showing strong agreement.

1. A: I heard you went to Vancouver last summer. That must have been fun.
   B: Definitely! It's one of my favorite cities in the world.
2. A: I love it when the train isn't that crowded.
   B: I couldn't agree more. It's much easier to get work done.

Ⓑ PAIRS Practice the conversations in 3A.

# 4 CONVERSATION

Ⓐ ▶07-10 Listen or watch. What do Gina and Elena mainly talk about?

Ⓑ ▶07-11 Listen or watch again. Answer the questions.

1. Where is Elena going next week?
2. What does Elena ask Gina?
3. What did Elena use to do every summer with her family in Peru?
4. What does Elena remember the most about her childhood trips?

Ⓒ ▶07-12 FOCUS ON LANGUAGE Listen or watch. Complete the conversation.

> Do you think Elena will decide to take the train or drive to Philadelphia? Give reasons.

> Gina: When I was a kid, my family _____ take the train to visit my grandparents in Chicago every year.
>
> Elena: Whoa! From New York? That must have been a long trip!
>
> Gina: _____ ! It took about 24 hours each way. But it was a lot of fun. We'd play card games for hours. When we got hungry, we'd eat in the dining _____ .
>
> Elena: That does sound fun.

# 5 TRY IT YOURSELF

Ⓐ THINK What is a trip you used to take? Complete the chart.

| | |
|---|---|
| Where would you go? | |
| How would you get there? | |
| What would you do? | |
| What do you remember the most? | |

Ⓑ PAIRS Student A: Share your travel story. Student B: Respond with an expression from 3A when you strongly agree with something. Use the conversation in 4C as an example.

Ⓒ REPORT Tell the class about your partner's travel story. Whose story is the most interesting? Whose is the funniest?

■ I CAN TALK ABOUT TRAVEL MEMORIES.

# LESSON 3 DISCUSS PAST TRANSPORTATION PREDICTIONS

**ELENA RUBIO**
@ElenaR

Just watched a talk about the kinds of transportation people thought we'd be using by now. There were some pretty strange ideas!

## 1 BEFORE YOU LISTEN

**A** Think of science fiction movies or TV shows you have seen. What kinds of technology do they predict there will be in the future?

**B** ▶07-13 VOCABULARY Listen. Then listen and repeat.

> **instantly:** immediately
> **predict:** to say what is going to happen before it happens
> **a prediction:** a statement saying what is going to happen before it happens
> **fascinate:** to interest someone very much
> **unrealistic:** not based on facts, not likely to happen
> **underestimate:** to think something is smaller or less important than it really is
> **urge:** to try hard to persuade someone to do something
> **a fad:** something that is popular for a short time

**C** Complete the sentences with words from 1B.

1. When we were kids, my friend made a silly _____ about the future, and this year it actually came true.
2. In the old days, it was hard for people to stay in touch, but now we can communicate _____ .
3. We often don't notice how fast things are changing, so we _____ how different the future will be.
4. When there's a new type of technology, it can be difficult to _____ if it will last or if it's just a(n) _____ .
5. It would be fun to have flying cars, but the idea is still pretty _____ .
6. The CEO held a meeting to _____ his employees to work harder and come up with some new ideas.
7. Movies about space travel _____ people of all ages.

## 2 GRAMMAR It + past passive

Use the past passive with *it* to describe past beliefs about the future.

| *It* + past passive | *That* | Subject | *Would* + verb | |
|---|---|---|---|---|
| It was thought | that | we | would have | flying cars soon. |
| It was believed | that | planes | would get | faster and faster. |
| It was expected | that | the airship | would be | a major form of transportation. |

**Note:** *It* + past passive is also used to describe beliefs in the past that are *not* about the future:
*It was believed that train travel was dangerous.*
*It was thought that the plane had crashed.*

>> FOR PRACTICE, GO TO PAGE 145

# 3 LISTENING

Adriana Lopez | TSW Global Speaker Program
Unit 7: Where's My Flying Car?

**A** ▶07-14 Listen or watch. What is the main idea of the talk?

**B** ▶07-15 Read the Listening Skill. Listen or watch again. Circle the correct adverb of degree to complete the sentence.

> **LISTENING SKILL** Listen for adverbs of degree
>
> Speakers often use adverbs of degree to strengthen or weaken a quality they are describing. These words can be an important clue to how strongly the speaker feels about a particular point.
>
> **Strengthening**            **Weakening**
> *extremely   really   quite*     *somewhat   a bit   fairly*

1. It's easy to be *a bit / quite* disappointed with our progress.
2. Maybe our ideas about flying have been *somewhat / extremely* unrealistic.
3. We need to be *fairly / really* careful about saying that things won't happen.

**C** ▶07-16 Listen or watch again. Complete the sentences with the correct type of transportation.

 helicopters   airplanes   wings   automobiles   airships   submarines

1. French artists imagined firefighters with _____ .
2. *Popular Mechanics* thought we would have personal _____ in our garages.
3. In the 1930s, people thought _____ would be a major form of transportation.
4. Supersonic _____ didn't succeed because they were too loud and expensive.
5. H.G. Wells said that we would never have _____ .
6. A well-known businessman said _____ were just a fad.

**D** VOCABULARY EXPANSION  Read each sentence from the talk. What do the underlined expressions mean?

1. If you grew up on science fiction, like I did, it's hard not to feel a little <u>let down</u> that we don't have all the cool stuff we've seen in the movies.

   _____

2. It was widely expected that super-fast planes would <u>take over</u> the airline industry.

   _____

3. Flights were too expensive and too loud. Because of these issues, supersonic flights <u>lost their appeal.</u>

   _____

**E** PAIRS  Compare your answers in 3D.

# 4 DISCUSSION

**A** THINK  What predictions about transportation, cities, homes, and the environment were made in the past? What is expected to happen now? Take notes.

**B** GROUPS  Share your predictions from 4A.

**C** EVALUATE  Report to the class. Have any of the past predictions come true? Do you think any others will? When?  ☐ I CAN DISCUSS PAST TRANSPORTATION PREDICTIONS.

ELENA RUBIO
@ElenaR

Can you imagine getting on an escalator that is 800 meters long?

## 1 BEFORE YOU READ

**A** PAIRS What are some of the ways you have traveled? Which ways were unusual?

**B** ▶07-17 VOCABULARY Listen. Then listen and repeat. Do you know these words?

| transport | mountainous | horizontal | escalator | practical | a commute | steep |

>> FOR DEFINITIONS AND PRACTICE, GO TO PAGE 145

## 2 READ

**A** PREVIEW Read the title and the subheadings. Look at the pictures. What do you think the article will be about?

**B** ▶07-18 Read and listen to the article. Was your prediction correct?

Home | Technology | Work | Social Media

# UNIQUE WAYS OF TRAVELING UP AND DOWN

Transportation usually moves people from side to side. Not every city, however, has the right conditions to transport everyone in this way. In places such as Hong Kong, Medellín, and Quebec City, urban planners have had to develop unique transportation systems that carry people mainly up and down.

5 **Hong Kong**

Hong Kong is an extremely mountainous city, so horizontal movement is limited. It took urban planners a while to find a solution to this problem. Finally, in 1993, they opened the Central-Mid-Levels escalator and moving walkway system. It connects the lower Central district of Hong Kong Island with the higher Mid-Levels district.

10 At 800 meters (2,600 feet) long, it is the largest outdoor covered escalator and moving walkway system in the world. It is lined with shops and restaurants, so it is not only a practical way to move people around, it is also a huge tourist attraction. In fact, it has been called one of the world's coolest commutes.

Central-Mid-Levels escalator and moving walkway system

**Medellín**

15 In Medellín, Colombia, the problem was slightly different. Urban planners needed to figure out how to help people who lived on the steep hills around the city. These people had a hard time making it down to the main part of the city for shopping, school, and work because there were so few public buses.

The solution turned out to be the Metrocable gondola system. Opened in 2004, 20 this transportation system connects people on the hillsides with other public transportation options in the city. It has already made a huge difference. The first line, Line K, carries about 30,000 people every day, and greatly reduces their commuting time. The city continues to add new lines to the system in order to increase the number of people it serves.

Metrocable gondola system

Old Quebec Funicular

25 **Quebec City**

In Quebec City, Canada, the problem was how to link two different parts of the city. Urban planners wanted to connect the Lower Town section with the Upper Town section. These two parts of the city are not far apart, but they are separated by a steep hill.

30 The Old Quebec Funicular became the solution to this problem. A funicular is a type of railroad that uses cables to move cars up and down. Serving both the residents of Quebec and tourists, it opened in 1879 as a water-powered system and switched to electric power in 1907. Despite stretching just 64 meters (210 feet), it rises 59 meters (194 feet) at a 45-degree angle, making it feel like an

35 amusement park ride. It gives people a fun, more relaxing way of getting from one part of the city to the other.

By 2050, experts predict that there will be 10 billion people on Earth and more than 6.5 billion of them will live in cities. This will create new challenges for the world's current transportation systems. It is likely that urban planners will have to come up with new systems to help everyone get around.

# 3 CHECK YOUR UNDERSTANDING

**A** Read the article again. What is the main idea?

**B** Answer the questions, according to the article.

1. Why can't transportation always move in a horizontal direction?

_____

2. What three transportation systems are described in the article?

_____

3. Why might urban planners have to develop new transportation systems in the future?

_____

**C** CLOSE READING Reread lines 2–3 in the article. Then circle the correct answer.

The three cities are examples of places that _____ .

a. can move everyone horizontally

b. can't move everyone horizontally

c. plan to move everyone horizontally

**D** Read the Reading Skill. Then reread the article and complete the chart.

| City | Problem | Transportation solution |
|---|---|---|
| Hong Kong | | |
| Medellín | | |
| Quebec City | | |

> **READING SKILL Identify problems and solutions**
>
> Writers often organize a text by mentioning a problem first and then giving the solution. They sometimes introduce problems and solutions with phrases such as *the problem was…* and *the solution turned out to be….*

**E** PAIRS What is the article about? Retell the most important ideas. Use your own words.

What new transportation systems are being developed in other cities?

# 4 MAKE IT PERSONAL

**A** THINK What are some of the problems with transportation where you live? How could they be solved? What are some unique solutions?

**B** PAIRS Share your ideas. Which solutions are the best? Which are the most realistic?

☐ I CAN READ ABOUT UNIQUE TRANSPORTATION SYSTEMS.

**ELENA RUBIO**
@ElenaR

Back from a marketing conference in Philadelphia. Met so many smart, interesting people.

## 1 BEFORE YOU WRITE

**A** When was the last time you sent someone a thank-you letter or email? Who was it to? Why did you write it?

**B** Read Elena's emails. How are they the same? How are they different?

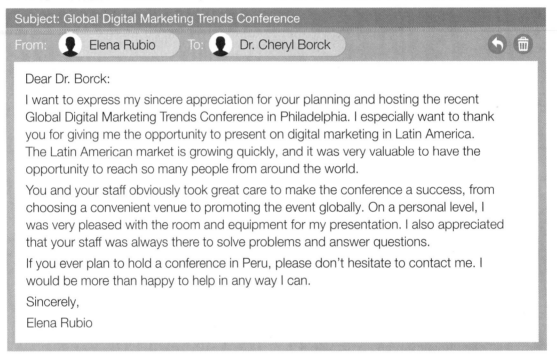

Subject: Global Digital Marketing Trends Conference

From: Elena Rubio    To: Dr. Cheryl Borck

Dear Dr. Borck:

I want to express my sincere appreciation for your planning and hosting the recent Global Digital Marketing Trends Conference in Philadelphia. I especially want to thank you for giving me the opportunity to present on digital marketing in Latin America. The Latin American market is growing quickly, and it was very valuable to have the opportunity to reach so many people from around the world.

You and your staff obviously took great care to make the conference a success, from choosing a convenient venue to promoting the event globally. On a personal level, I was very pleased with the room and equipment for my presentation. I also appreciated that your staff was always there to solve problems and answer questions.

If you ever plan to hold a conference in Peru, please don't hesitate to contact me. I would be more than happy to help in any way I can.

Sincerely,

Elena Rubio

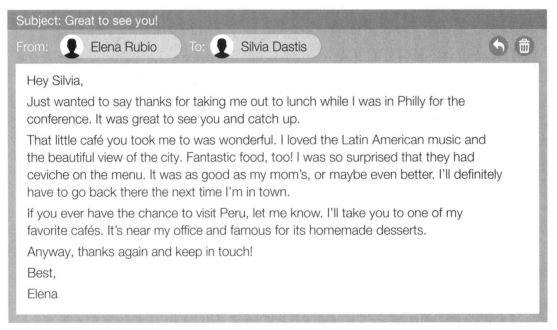

Subject: Great to see you!

From: Elena Rubio    To: Silvia Dastis

Hey Silvia,

Just wanted to say thanks for taking me out to lunch while I was in Philly for the conference. It was great to see you and catch up.

That little café you took me to was wonderful. I loved the Latin American music and the beautiful view of the city. Fantastic food, too! I was so surprised that they had ceviche on the menu. It was as good as my mom's, or maybe even better. I'll definitely have to go back there the next time I'm in town.

If you ever have the chance to visit Peru, let me know. I'll take you to one of my favorite cafés. It's near my office and famous for its homemade desserts.

Anyway, thanks again and keep in touch!

Best,

Elena

**C** Read the emails again. Complete the chart.

| Parts of the emails | Email #1 | Email #2 |
|---|---|---|
| Greeting | | Hey Silvia, |
| Main reason for saying thanks | planning and hosting a conference | |
| Details for saying thanks | | Latin American music, beautiful view, fantastic food |
| Closing | Sincerely, Elena Rubio | |

## 2 FOCUS ON WRITING

Read the Writing Skill. Then reread the first email. Underline the formal expressions in the email that have the same meaning as the informal expressions below.

1. Thank you so much for organizing the conference…
2. Thanks for letting me present…
3. …it was great to get the chance…
4. You and your staff made sure the conference went well…
5. your staff was always there to help…

> **WRITING SKILL  Choose the right level of formality**
>
> Think about who you are writing to and why you are writing to this person. This will help you to decide whether to use formal or informal language. Formal writing usually has full sentences and more professional greetings and closings. It usually does not have contractions or emotional language.

## 3 PLAN YOUR WRITING

**A** THINK  Who is someone you could send a thank-you email to? Why could you thank this person? Draw a chart like the one in 1C.

**B** PAIRS  Talk about who you could thank and why you could thank this person.

## 4 WRITE

Write a thank-you email to the person you chose in 3A. Include a main reason for saying thanks and specific details. Use the right level of formality. Choose one of the emails in 1B as a model.

## 5 REVISE YOUR WRITING

**A** PAIRS  Exchange emails and read each other's writing.
1. Did your partner include a main reason for saying thanks and specific details?
2. Did your partner use the right level of formality?

> **Writing tip**
> Read your first draft out loud several times. This will help you know if it sounds too formal or informal.

**B** PAIRS  Can your partner improve his or her email? Make suggestions.

## 6 PROOFREAD

Read your email again. Check your
- spelling
- punctuation
- capitalization

▮ I CAN WRITE A THANK-YOU EMAIL.

# PUT IT TOGETHER

## 1 PRESENTATION PROJECT

**A** ▶07-19 Listen or watch. What is the topic of the presentation?

**B** ▶07-20 Listen or watch again. Answer the questions.

1. How does Junio describe the place in the presentation?

_____

2. What three activities does Junio recommend doing there?

_____

**C** Read the presentation skill. How can this skill help your audience?

**D** Make your own presentation.

**Step 1** Think about a place that you are interested in or have visited. Recommend three activities your classmates should do there.

**Step 2** Prepare a two-minute presentation about the activities you recommend. Bring an item or picture that is related to the place or activities.

> **PRESENTATION SKILL**
> **Repeat your main ideas**
> To emphasize the most important points of your presentation, say them more than once.

**Step 3** Give your presentation to the class. Remember to use the presentation skill. Answer questions and get feedback.

How did you do? Complete the self-evaluation on page 165.

## 2 REFLECT AND PLAN

**A** Look back through the unit. Check (✓) the things you learned. Highlight the things you need to learn.

**Speaking objectives**
- ☐ Talk about air travel preferences
- ☐ Talk about travel memories
- ☐ Discuss past transportation predictions

**Vocabulary**
- ☐ Air travel terms
- ☐ Train and car travel terms

**Conversation**
- ☐ Show strong agreement

**Pronunciation**
- ☐ Reduced pronunciation of *than*

**Listening**
- ☐ Listen for adverbs of degree

**Grammar**
- ☐ Comparisons with gerund and noun phrases
- ☐ Past habits with *would / used to*
- ☐ *It* + past passive

**Reading**
- ☐ Identify problems and solutions

**Writing**
- ☐ Choose the right level of formality

**B** What will you do to learn the things you highlighted? For example, use your app, review your Student Book, or do other practice. Make a plan.

❮ Notes          Done

In the app, do the Lesson 3 Listening activities: Discuss past transportation predictions

_____

_____

_____

_____

# 8 HOW HAVE YOU BEEN?

## LEARNING GOALS

In this unit, you
- ⊘ talk about interacting with people
- ⊘ talk about self-improvement
- ⊘ discuss your bucket list
- ⊘ read about overcoming rejection
- ⊘ write a narrative

## GET STARTED

**A** Read the unit title and learning goals.

**B** Look at the photo. What's going on?

**C** Now read Michael's message. How does he feel?

**MICHAEL STEWART**
@MichaelS

I've always believed that we don't learn from experience—we learn from reflecting on experience.

**MICHAEL STEWART**

@MichaelS

Just had a difficult meeting with a new client. May have to start over on this project.

 **1 VOCABULARY** Ways of behaving

**A** ▶08-01 **Listen. Then listen and repeat.**

> **keep your cool:** to stay calm and focused in a difficult situation
> **make fun of:** to make unkind jokes about someone or something
> **lose your temper:** to become very angry, usually suddenly
> **be hard on:** to treat someone in an unfair way or be too strict
> **talk back:** to answer a parent or a teacher in a rude way
> **raise your voice:** to speak loudly because you are angry
> **overreact:** to respond too strongly or emotionally to a situation
> **talk it over:** to discuss something with someone to help you decide what to do
> **work it out:** to find a solution to a problem by thinking about it carefully
> **deal with:** to do something about a problem

**B** Write the words from 1A in the correct column.

| Appropriate behavior | Inappropriate behavior |
|---|---|
|  |  |

**C** PAIRS Talk about times when the words in 1A described your behavior.

## 2 GRAMMAR Modals for past regrets and possibilities

Use *should have* to talk about past regrets. Use *could have, may have,* and *might have* to talk about past possibilities.

| Statements | | | | |
|---|---|---|---|---|
| **Subject** | **Modal** | **(Not)** | **Have** | **Past participle** |
| I | should could may might | (not) | have | kept | my cool. |

| Questions | | | |
|---|---|---|---|
| **Modal** | **Subject** | **Have** | **Past participle** |
| Should Could | they | have | kept | their cool? |

**Notes**
- In spoken English, we often use the contractions *should've, could've,* and *might've.*
- We also use contractions for the negative form of *shouldn't have* and *couldn't have.*
- We don't use a contraction for the negative form of *may not* or *might not.*
- We don't form questions with *may...have* or *might...have.*

**>> FOR PRACTICE, GO TO PAGE 146**

## 3 CONVERSATION SKILL

**A** ▶08-02 Read the conversation skill. Listen. Notice how the speaker acknowledges a mistake.

1. A: Did you send in your report yet?
   B: Oh. I have to admit that I forgot to turn it in. I'm so sorry!
2. A: Is this the right meeting room?
   B: No. I messed up. I booked the wrong one.

**B** PAIRS Practice the conversations in 3A.

| Acknowledge a mistake | |
|---|---|
| In addition to saying that we're sorry, we can use these expressions to admit that we made a mistake. | |
| **More informal** | **More formal** |
| *I messed up.* | *That's my fault.* |
| *That's on me.* | *I have to admit that…* |
| *I know I messed up.* | *I take the blame for that.* |

## 4 CONVERSATION

**A** ▶08-03 Listen or watch. What do Michael and Elena talk about?

**B** ▶08-04 Listen or watch again. Answer the questions.

1. What is Michael doing when Elena greets him?
2. What happened after Michael sent the schedule?
3. Why did the client have a right to be angry?
4. Why does Elena say, "You live and learn"?

What do you think Michael learned from his experience?

**C** ▶08-05 FOCUS ON LANGUAGE Listen or watch. Complete the conversation.

Michael: I had a tough meeting with a client this morning.

Elena: Oh?

Michael: Yeah, I was supposed to send him the schedule for our new project. I thought I'd emailed everything last week, but it was still in my drafts folder. He was furious.

Elena: Oh, no. So how'd you _____ it?

Michael: Of course, I apologized and promised to get him the information right away. I felt bad. I mean, I really _____ . I _____ been more organized.

## 5 TRY IT YOURSELF

**A** THINK Read the scenarios. How could you handle these situations? Take notes.

| 1 Customer | 2 Co-worker | 3 Family member |
|---|---|---|
| An angry customer upset you and you lost your cool. The customer complained about you. What should you say to your manager? | A new co-worker asked for help, but you said you were too busy. Now, the co-worker isn't very friendly with you. What can you say to make the relationship better? | You and your cousin were joking around. Your cousin said something mean and you lost your temper. Now, your cousin isn't talking to you. What should you say to your cousin? |

**B** PAIRS Discuss what you could have, should have, or might have done differently for each scenario and acknowledge your mistake.

**C** EVALUATE Discuss the different responses to the scenarios. Which ones are better than others?

■ I CAN TALK ABOUT INTERACTING WITH PEOPLE.

**MICHAEL STEWART**
@MichaelS

It's hard to find time to work on my Chinese grammar. Not enough hours in the day!

## 1 VOCABULARY  Self-improvement language

**A** ▶08-06 Listen. Then listen and repeat.

> **become fluent in:** to begin to be able to speak or read a language very well
> **become more skilled at:** to begin to have the ability to do something very well
> **get a feel for:** to familiarize yourself with something
> **master:** to learn a skill or language so well you can do it easily
> **commit to:** to say you will definitely do something
> **get a handle on:** to start to understand a situation or how to do something
> **excel in:** to do something very well
> **devote more time to:** to spend more time doing something

**B** What are the steps of the learning process? Complete the chart with the words and phrases from 1A. Some can go in more than one column.

| At the beginning | During | At the end |
| --- | --- | --- |
|  |  |  |

**C** PAIRS Talk about three things you would like to get better at or learn. Use words from 1A.

## 2 GRAMMAR  *Wish* and *if only*: Review and expand

Use *wish* and *if only* to express regrets and wishes for the past, present, and future.

| **Present wishes** | | | | |
| --- | --- | --- | --- | --- |
| He wishes (that) If only | he |  | devoted | more time to studying. |
| He wishes (that) If only |  | could | devote | |
| **Future wishes** | | | | |
| They wish (that) If only | they | could would | devote | more time to studying next year. |
| **Past wishes / regrets** | | | | |
| I wish (that) If only | I |  | had devoted | more time to studying. |
| I wish (that) If only |  | could | have devoted | |

**Notes**
- *If only* expresses a stronger meaning than *I wish*.
- We use *if only* to say we would really like things to be different.

**>> FOR PRACTICE, GO TO PAGE 147**

# 3 PRONUNCIATION

**A** ▶08-07 Read and listen to the pronunciation note.

**B** ▶08-08 Listen. Notice how the vowels are linked.

| /y/ | /w/ |
|---|---|
| quiᵞet, areᵞa, reᵞality | fluʷent, poʷetry, coʷoperate |
| _____ _____ _____ | _____ _____ _____ |

**C** ▶08-09 Listen. Add each word to the correct column in 3B.

1. variety
2. client
3. situation
4. fluids
5. diet
6. influence

**D** PAIRS Practice the words from 3B and 3C.

# 4 CONVERSATION

**A** ▶08-10 Listen or watch. What do Michael and Elena talk about?

**B** ▶08-11 Listen or watch again. Answer the questions.

1. What is Michael trying to learn?
2. What advice does Elena give Michael?
3. What has Elena always wanted to do?
4. What would be a dream come true for Elena?

Do you think Michael and Elena will achieve their goals? Why or why not?

**C** ▶08-12 FOCUS ON LANGUAGE Listen or watch. Complete the conversation.

**Michael:** I've been studying Mandarin for a few months now. I'm planning to visit China next summer, and I'd like to be able to speak at least a little bit of the language while I'm there.

**Elena:** Wow! I'm impressed! I've heard Mandarin can be a tough language to _____ .

**Michael:** Yeah. It's something I've always wanted to learn. But to be honest, I've been struggling to get a handle on it.

**Elena:** Well, I imagine it takes a lot of practice to become _____ .

**Michael:** Right. There are so many characters to memorize. I just _____ I could devote more time to it.

# 5 TRY IT YOURSELF

**A** THINK What are three of your goals? What do you wish you could do now to achieve them? What do you wish you had done in the past to help you achieve them? Take notes.

**B** PAIRS Share your goals and wishes. Give each other advice. Use the conversation in 4C as an example.

**C** REPORT Tell your classmates about your partner's goals. What are some popular goals? What are some common wishes?

■ I CAN TALK ABOUT SELF-IMPROVEMENT.

**MICHAEL STEWART**

@MichaelS

Just watched a talk about bucket lists. I have so many ideas for mine!

## 1 BEFORE YOU LISTEN

**A** What are some of your goals and dreams? Which ones have you already achieved?

**B** ▶08-13 VOCABULARY Listen. Then listen and repeat.

> **spontaneous:** doing things without planning or organizing them first
> **determined:** having a strong desire to do something even when it is difficult
> **an excursion:** a short trip
> **accomplish:** to succeed in doing something
> **an inspiration:** something that encourages you to do something good
> **fulfilling:** making you feel happy or satisfied because you are doing interesting or important things
> **an ambition:** a strong desire to do or achieve something

**C** Complete the sentences with words from 1B.

1. That book was a big _____ to me. It made me want to do good things with my life.
2. On my tour, we went on a quick _____ into the mountains one day.
3. My only real _____ is to enjoy my life as much as I can.
4. Sometimes I like to be _____ and try something new without having a reason.
5. It's not easy to master a new language, but I'm _____ to speak English fluently.
6. There are so many things that I want to _____ in my life that I don't think I'll be able to do them all.
7. His job pays well, but it's not _____ . He doesn't seem very happy to go to work every day.

## 2 GRAMMAR Comparisons between clauses

Use *more than* or *less than* to set up a comparison between two clauses.

| Clause | *More / less than* | Clause |
|---|---|---|
| You might enjoy your unplanned excursions | more than | you enjoy the view from the Eiffel Tower. |
| I want to have fulfilling life experiences | more than | I want to travel to new places. |
| He cares about studying | less than | he cares about seeing the world. |

Notes

- In shorter comparisons, we sometimes delete part of the second clause to avoid repetition:
  *You might enjoy your unplanned excursions more than (you enjoy) the view from the Eiffel Tower.*
  *He cares about studying less than (he cares about) seeing the world.*
- In shorter comparisons, we also often use auxiliary verbs to avoid repetition:
  *We care about having fun more than he **does**.*

>> FOR PRACTICE, GO TO PAGE 148

## 3 LISTENING

**A** ▶08-14 Listen or watch. What is the main idea of the talk?

**B** ▶08-15 Read the Listening Skill. Listen or watch again. How does the speaker define or explain the following phrases?

1. kicks the bucket

   _____

2. less spontaneous

   _____

3. things I know I can do

   _____

Kendrick Scott / TSW Global Speaker Program
**Unit 8: Making a Bucket List**

> **LISTENING SKILL** Listen for explanations
>
> Speakers often define or explain a word or idea in the phrase or sentence that comes after it. They don't always use expressions like *meaning* or *which means* to introduce these explanations.

**C** ▶08-16 Listen or watch again. Answer the questions.

1. What made the idea of bucket lists more popular?

   _____

2. What can be two problems with making a bucket list?

   _____

3. What are two things on the speaker's bucket list?

   _____

4. What are two ideas that people can find online?

   _____

**D** VOCABULARY EXPANSION  Read each sentence from the talk. What do the underlined expressions mean?

1. I <u>got it into my head</u> that I had to see Paris from the top of the Eiffel Tower.

   _____

2. I'm sure I missed out on taking some interesting <u>side trips</u> that could have come up along the way.

   _____

3. I always <u>keep in mind</u> that my list is a guide, a reminder of my dreams and ambitions.

   _____

**E** PAIRS  Compare answers in 3D.

## 4 DISCUSSION

**A** THINK  What five things would you put on your bucket list? Take notes.

**B** DISCUSS  In small groups, share your bucket lists. Discuss which items on the lists are the most important to you.

I want to walk on the Great Wall of China more than I want to visit Berlin.

**C** ANALYZE  Report to the class. Put the most important bucket-list items into these categories: travel, learning, family, work, other. Which category has the most items?

■ I CAN DISCUSS MY BUCKET LIST.

**MICHAEL STEWART**
@MichaelS

I used to fear being rejected! But as I've gotten older I care about it much less.

## 1 BEFORE YOU READ

**A** PAIRS In what situations might people feel rejected?

**B** ▶08-17 VOCABULARY Listen. Then listen and repeat. Do you know these words?

| rejection | assume | overcome | an entrepreneur | pursue | therapy | profound |

>> FOR DEFINITIONS AND PRACTICE, GO TO PAGE 148

## 2 READ

**A** PREVIEW Read the title and look at the photo. What do you think the article will be about?

**B** ▶08-18 Read and listen to the article. Was your prediction correct?

### Rejection Isn't Always a
# TERRIBLE THING

Everyone hates being rejected, whether it's for a job, a university, or even a date. It's easy to assume that you were turned down because you weren't qualified enough, smart enough, or
5 good-looking enough. Most of the time we run away from rejection, never knowing the real reason for it. According to author and presenter Jia Jiang, however, we can overcome it. We can also turn it into a powerful tool that can make our lives better.

10 Jiang had his first experience with rejection when he was growing up in China. At the age of six, he was one of only three children in his class not to be chosen to receive a special gift. This experience hurt him deeply and made him never want to be
15 rejected again. When Jiang was fourteen, Bill Gates came and spoke at his school, inspiring him to become a successful entrepreneur. He moved to the United States a couple of years later, eager to pursue his dream. By the age of thirty, however,
20 he was no closer to his goal of becoming a global business leader. When he thought about it, he realized that he was always stopped from doing something important by his fear of rejection.

One day, while searching for a solution to his
25 problem on the internet, he found a website called Rejection Therapy. It suggested that people could overcome their fear of rejection by going out and looking for it. He loved this idea and decided to get rejected once a day for 100 days in a row. He made a
30 list of 100 simple ways to get rejected and filmed his experiences.

Two of the experiences in particular had a profound impact on him. On one of the
35 first days, he went to a donut shop and asked to have donuts made in the shape of the Olympic rings. He was shocked
40 and touched when the donut maker actually took him seriously and fulfilled his request. Another day, he went to a stranger's house and asked to plant a flower in the stranger's backyard. When the stranger said no, he stayed and asked
45 why. The stranger explained that he had a dog that liked to dig things up. He recommended that Jiang talk to another neighbor who loved flowers instead. Jiang realized that by talking to the stranger he was able to negotiate with him and gain his trust.

50 Through his project, Jiang learned that he didn't need to run away from rejection. In fact, if he stayed and talked, he could turn the rejection into a powerful learning experience. He also discovered that people were often a lot kinder than he had
55 thought.

After the project, Jiang took over the Rejection Therapy website. He also started writing and speaking about his experiences. Since then, he has helped many people to see rejection differently and
60 sometimes even overcome it to get what they want.

## 3 CHECK YOUR UNDERSTANDING

**Ⓐ** Read the article again. What is the main idea?

**Ⓑ** Answer the questions, according to the article.

1.  Why wasn't Jiang ever able to do anything important?

    _____

2.  How did Jiang try to overcome his fear of rejection?

    _____

3.  What did Jiang learn from trying to get rejected?

    _____

4.  How is Jiang trying to help others overcome their fear of rejection?

    _____

**Ⓒ** CLOSE READING  Reread lines 5–9 in the article. Then circle the correct answers.

1.  What does the word *it* refer to in each of the three sentences?
    a.  rejection
    b.  Jia Jiang's fear of rejection
    c.  a tool that can make our lives better
2.  What can we infer about Jia Jiang?
    a.  He has already learned how to overcome rejection.
    b.  He still wants to discover how to overcome rejection.
    c.  He does not think that anyone can overcome rejection.

**Ⓓ** Read the Reading Skill. Then reread the article and circle the correct answers.

| READING SKILL |
| --- |
| **Notice transitions between paragraphs** |
| Writers use transitions to connect paragraphs and keep their ideas and information flowing smoothly. Sometimes they make transitions by using words and phrases that show things like sequence, addition, and contrast. Other times, they repeat a word, concept, or idea from the previous paragraph. |

1.  How is the transition shown between paragraph 3 and paragraph 4?
    a.  by using a phrase to show contrast
    b.  by repeating the word *experiences*
    c.  by repeating the concept of filming
2.  How is the transition shown between paragraphs 5 and 6?
    a.  by repeating the name *Jiang*
    b.  by repeating the website's name
    c.  by using a phrase to show sequence

**Ⓔ** PAIRS  What is the article about? Retell the most important ideas. Use your own words.

> How else did Jiang try to get rejected? 🔍

## 4 MAKE IT PERSONAL

**Ⓐ** THINK  What do you think of Jiang's experiment for overcoming rejection? Would you try something like this? What else could you do to overcome rejection?

**Ⓑ** PAIRS  Share your ideas. Which are some of the best ways to overcome rejection?

*I think that one of the easiest ways to overcome rejection is to talk things over with a friend or family member. The people closest to you can help you feel better and put things in perspective.*

■ I CAN READ ABOUT OVERCOMING REJECTION.

**MICHAEL STEWART**
@MichaelS

A decision I made in college changed my life forever. Read my blog about it!

## 1 BEFORE YOU WRITE

**A** How do you make important decisions? Is there anyone you ask for help?

**B** Complete the sentences with the words in the box.

> tryout     rapid     stable

1. They want him to work here until he retires, so his job is very _____
2. The coach held a _____ to see who was good enough to be on the team.
3. It is hard to keep up with all the _____ changes in technology.

**C** Read the blog. What important decision did Michael make?

About | Contact       Search

## No Regrets

I love my job! Even after many years, I still look forward to going to the office and working with my amazing teammates every day. Sometimes, though, I think about that day years ago when I made a decision that changed my life forever.

When I was in high school, my passion was playing hockey. In my senior year, my team won the championship, and I scored the winning goal. I was the school hero! I continued to play on a team at university, and I really enjoyed the challenge. I guess I was pretty good since just before graduation, a professional hockey team called and invited me to have a tryout. The only thing I had to do was call the team back and schedule a date. At first, I was really excited, but then I started to have second thoughts. I had already been offered a great job at a new marketing firm that could launch my career. Several times, I picked up the phone to call, but then I stopped. In the end, I never called the hockey team back.

Sometimes I think about how different my life would have been if I had become a professional hockey player. But then I remember that if I had become a big star, I might not have gotten the great job I have today. I like that my current career is stable, while at the same time, the rapid changes in digital technology always challenge me to learn new things. I know that I can grow and advance in my work for years to come.

As much as I like to imagine myself as a great hockey player, I know deep down that I wasn't really that good. Maybe I should have called the team back and gone to the tryout, but I can't change the past, and it's always better to look forward in life. Sure, I'll always wonder what could have happened, but I'll never regret the decision I made to be part of the team I'm on today.

**D** Read the blog again. Complete the chart.

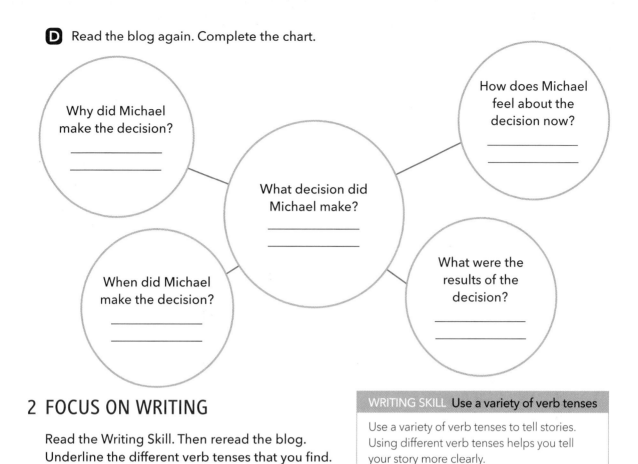

Why did Michael make the decision?
_____
_____

What decision did Michael make?
_____
_____

How does Michael feel about the decision now?
_____
_____

When did Michael make the decision?
_____
_____

What were the results of the decision?
_____
_____

## 2 FOCUS ON WRITING

Read the Writing Skill. Then reread the blog. Underline the different verb tenses that you find.

> **WRITING SKILL   Use a variety of verb tenses**
>
> Use a variety of verb tenses to tell stories. Using different verb tenses helps you tell your story more clearly.

## 3 PLAN YOUR WRITING

**A** THINK  What important decision has affected your life? Draw a chart like the one in 1D.

**B** PAIRS  Talk about your important decision and how it has affected your life.

## 4 WRITE

Write a blog about an important decision that has affected your life. Include a variety of verb tenses. Use the blog in 1C as a model.

> **Pre-writing tip**
>
> Free write for a while before you start your first draft. When you free write, you don't worry about organization or grammar. This will help you come up with ideas for your first draft.

## 5 REVISE YOUR WRITING

**A** PAIRS  Exchange blogs and read each other's writing.

1. Did your partner clearly explain the decision and how it has affected his or her life?
2. Did your partner use a variety of verb tenses?

**B** PAIRS  Can your partner improve his or her blog? Make suggestions.

## 6 PROOFREAD

Read your blog again. Check your

- spelling
- punctuation
- capitalization

■ I CAN WRITE A NARRATIVE.

# PUT IT TOGETHER

## 1 PRESENTATION PROJECT

**A** ▶08-19 Listen or watch. What is the topic of the presentation?

**B** ▶08-20 Listen or watch again. Answer the questions.

1. Who challenged Misaki to achieve this goal?

   _____

2. What did Misaki have to do to achieve this goal?

   _____

3. How did Misaki feel about achieving the goal?

   _____

**C** Read the presentation skill. How can this make you a better speaker?

**D** Make your own presentation.

**Step 1** Think of a goal you have achieved. How did you achieve it? How did you feel about achieving it?

**Step 2** Prepare a two-minute presentation about the goal you achieved. Bring an item or picture that is related to it.

**Step 3** Give your presentation to the class. Remember to use the presentation skill. Answer questions and get feedback.

> **PRESENTATION SKILL**
>
> **Sound conversational**
> Although you should practice what you are going to say, you should not sound like you are reading from a script.

How did you do? Complete the self-evaluation on page 165.

## 2 REFLECT AND PLAN

**A** Look back through the unit. Check (✓) the things you learned. Highlight the things you need to learn.

**Speaking objectives**
- ☐ Talk about interacting with people
- ☐ Talk about self-improvement
- ☐ Discuss your bucket list

**Vocabulary**
- ☐ Ways of behaving
- ☐ Self-improvement language

**Conversation**
- ☐ Acknowledge a mistake

**Pronunciation**
- ☐ Link vowels within a word

**Listening**
- ☐ Listen for explanations

**Grammar**
- ☐ Modals for past regrets and possibilities
- ☐ *Wish* and *if only*
- ☐ Comparisons between clauses

**Reading**
- ☐ Notice transitions between paragraphs

**Writing**
- ☐ Use a variety of verb tenses

**B** What will you do to learn the things you highlighted? For example, use your app, review your Student Book, or do other practice. Make a plan.

Notes | Done

Review the Lesson 1 Vocabulary: Ways of behaving, page 90.

_____

_____

_____

# WOULD YOU MIND HELPING ME?

LEARNING GOALS

In this unit, you
- ⊘ ask for help and show appreciation
- ⊘ talk about possible changes at work
- ⊘ discuss ways to solve problems
- ⊘ read about finding a job
- ⊘ write a letter of recommendation

## GET STARTED

**A** Read the unit title and learning goals.

**B** Look at the photo. What's going on?

**C** Now read Hana's message. How does she feel?

**HANA LEE**
@HanaL

So excited for a new challenge. I'm lucky to have supportive co-workers on my side.

**HANA LEE**
@HanaL

Working on my application for business school. Anyone know a good editor?

## 1 VOCABULARY
Elements of the writing process

**A** ▶09-01 Listen. Then listen and repeat.

> **submit:** to turn in a piece of writing for it to be checked or approved
> **double-check:** to look at something again so you are sure about it
> **draft:** to write something that you plan to change before it is finished
> **edit:** to improve a piece of writing by removing mistakes and making other changes
> **revise:** to change a piece of writing by making improvements or correcting mistakes
> **look over:** to check something quickly
> **organize:** to put things into an order or system
> **brainstorm:** to think of different ideas or ways to do something
> **give feedback:** to give your opinion about something

**B** What are the steps of the writing process? Complete the timeline with the verbs from 1A in the order you would use them.

**The Writing Process**

| Beginning | Middle | End |
|---|---|---|

submit

## 2 GRAMMAR   *Would / Do you mind* for permission and requests

Use *Would you mind if…?* and *Do you mind if…?* to politely ask for permission.
Use *Would you mind* + gerund…? and *Do you mind* + gerund…? to make polite requests.

| Ask for permission | | | | |
|---|---|---|---|---|
| ***Would / Do you mind*** | ***If*** | | **Verb** | |
| Would you mind | if | I | made | a suggestion? |
| Do you mind | | | make | |

**Notes**
- *Would you mind…?* is more polite than *Do you mind…?*
- Use the simple past with *Would you mind…?* and the simple present with *Do you mind…?*
- Even though the simple past is used with *Would you mind…?*, the request is for the present or future.
- In informal English we sometimes use the simple present with *Would you mind…?*

| Make a request | | |
|---|---|---|
| ***Would / Do you mind*** | **Gerund** | |
| Would / Do you mind | looking over | what I've written? |

**Notes**
- Use the negative form to politely ask someone to stop doing something:
  *Would you mind not talking during the presentation?*
- To accept a polite request, say: *No, I don't mind* or *Not at all.*
- To decline a polite request, say: *I'm sorry, but…*; *I'd like to, but…*; or *I wish I could, but….*

**>> FOR PRACTICE, GO TO PAGE 149**

# 3 CONVERSATION SKILL

**A** ▶09-02 Read the conversation skill. Listen. Notice how the speaker expresses appreciation.

1. A: Hey! I just finished looking over your paper. It looks great!
   B: Thanks.
2. A: I revised the report.
   B: Thank you very much. I really appreciate your help.

**B** PAIRS Practice the conversations in 3A.

## Express appreciation

When someone helps us, we can say, *Thank you* or *Thank you very much*. We can also use these other expressions:

| More informal | More formal |
|---|---|
| *Thanks.* | *Thank you so much for your help.* |
| *Thanks a lot.* | |
| *That's really helpful.* | *Thank you for taking the time to help me.* |
| *Thanks for your time / help.* | *I'm really grateful for everything you have done.* |
| | *I really appreciate your help.* |

# 4 CONVERSATION

**A** ▶09-03 Listen or watch. What do Gina and Hana talk about?

**B** ▶09-04 Listen or watch again. Answer the questions.

1. What is Hana doing when Gina starts talking to her?
2. Why is Hana applying to graduate school?
3. What advice does Gina give Hana about her application essay?
4. What does Gina offer to do after Hana revises her application essay?

> How would you describe the relationship between Hana and Gina? Do they seem to get along well?

**C** ▶09-05 FOCUS ON LANGUAGE Listen or watch. Complete the conversation.

Hana: I'm still waiting for a couple of letters of recommendation, and I need to finish this application essay.

Gina: Oh, those things are so hard to write. Is there anything I can help you with?

Hana: Well, actually, could you do me a big favor? _____ looking over these two paragraphs and giving me some _____ ?

Gina: No, not at all. I'd be happy to.

Hana: _____ . I really appreciate it.

# 5 TRY IT YOURSELF

**A** THINK Imagine that you need help with writing an application for a school program or a job. Complete the chart.

| What are you writing? | Why are you writing it? | What do you want help with? |
|---|---|---|
| | | |

**B** ROLE PLAY Student A: Politely ask for help with your writing and express appreciation. Student B: Agree to help and offer suggestions. Use the conversation in 4C as an example.

**C** REPORT Present your writing requests to the class. Which part of the writing process do most people want help with?

☐ I CAN ASK FOR HELP AND SHOW APPRECIATION.

# TALK ABOUT POSSIBLE CHANGES AT WORK

**HANA LEE**
@HanaL

Big meeting at work today.
Wonder what it's all about.

 **1 VOCABULARY** Employment terms

**A** ▶09-06 Listen. Then listen and repeat.

> **hire:** to pay someone to do work
> **fire:** to force someone to leave his or her job
> **promote:** to give someone a more important job
> **retire:** to stop working, usually because of old age
> **resign:** to officially leave your job because you want to
> **lay off:** to end someone's job because there is not enough work
> **transfer:** to move someone from one job or department to another
> **eliminate:** to completely get rid of something, like a specific job or role
> **assign:** to give someone a particular job or responsibility

**B** Complete the chart with words from 1A.

| Positive | Sometimes positive or negative | Negative |
|---|---|---|
| | | |

**C** PAIRS Discuss your answers in 1B. Explain your choices.

## 2 GRAMMAR Modals with the passive

We can use modals with the passive to talk about what is possible or expected in the near future.

| Statements | | | | |
|---|---|---|---|---|
| **Subject** | **Modal** | **(Not)** | **Passive** | |
| | | | **Base form of the verb** | **Past participle** | |
| Some people | could should might | (not) | be | laid off. |
| | | | | assigned | to different teams. |

| Questions | | | | |
|---|---|---|---|---|
| **Modal** | **Subject** | **Passive** | | |
| | | **Base form of the verb** | **Past participle** | |
| Could Should Might | she | be | transferred | to a different department? |

>> **FOR PRACTICE, GO TO PAGE 150**

# 3 PRONUNCIATION

**A** ▶09-07 Read and listen to the pronunciation note.

> **Intonation in lists**
>
> Use *and* and *or* to join words into lists.
> The voice usually rises on the first word(s) in the list and falls on the last word.
> If the list can continue, use rising intonation and omit *and* or *or*: *Seoul, Lima, Beijing...*

**B** ▶09-08 Listen. Notice the intonation in the lists. Then listen and repeat.

1. People could be transferred, assigned to new offices, or even laid off.
2. The company will invest more in product development, research, training…

**C** ▶09-09 Listen. If the list is finished, draw a downward arrow (↘). If the list could continue, draw an upward arrow (↗). Then listen and repeat.

1. Paris, Tokyo, New York _____
2. hiring, firing, promotions _____
3. resign, retire, transfer _____
4. directors, managers, employees _____

**D** PAIRS Practice the lists in 3B and 3C.

# 4 CONVERSATION

**A** ▶09-10 Listen or watch. What did Gina and Hana just learn?

**B** ▶09-11 Listen or watch again. Answer the questions.

1. Why does Hana think the meeting is interesting?
2. Why isn't Gina interested in working in another country?
3. Why does Hana think working in another country could be a good idea?
4. When could Hana and Gina be given more information about the changes?

> How do you think Hana feels about the company changes? How about Gina?

**C** ▶09-12 FOCUS ON LANGUAGE Listen or watch. Complete the conversation.

| | |
|---|---|
| Hana: | Did you know about the new office opening up in Turkey? |
| Gina: | No, I didn't. But I think it's a good idea. We do a lot of business there. |
| Hana: | Do you think this will affect any of us? |
| Gina: | Well, there'll be a lot of work for those of us in HR. New people will have to be interviewed, _____ , and trained. |
| Hana: | Do you think some people _____ transferred there, too? |
| Gina: | It's possible. |

# 5 TRY IT YOURSELF

**A** THINK Read the case studies. What changes could be made at each company? Take notes.

| Case Study 1 | Case Study 2 |
|---|---|
| Company A wants to reorganize its staff to save money and make it more efficient. | Company B wants to expand to several new countries. |

**B** PAIRS Share your ideas. Use the conversation in 4C as an example.

**C** COMPARE Tell the class about your ideas. Do most people agree? Does anyone have experience with company changes? What happened?

■ I CAN TALK ABOUT POSSIBLE CHANGES AT WORK.

# LESSON 3    DISCUSS WAYS TO SOLVE PROBLEMS

### HANA LEE
@HanaL

This talk reminds me of my first boss. He described problems as "wake-up calls for creativity."

## 1 BEFORE YOU LISTEN

**A** What kinds of problems do people in different jobs have to solve? For example, an architect, a chef, or a store manager?

**B** ▶09-13 VOCABULARY Listen. Then listen and repeat.

> **turn to:** to go to someone or something for help
> **barely:** in a way that almost does not happen, exist
> **occur to:** to suddenly come into your mind
> **analyze:** to examine or think about something carefully in order to understand it
> **maintain:** to make something continue the same way as before
> **seek:** to try to find something
> **a mentor:** an experienced person who advises and helps a less experienced person
> **relate:** to be connected to something in some way

**C** Complete the sentences with words from 1B.

1. My manager taught me a lot about this job. She was a great _____ .
2. Could you speak a little louder? I can _____ hear you.
3. We all _____ solutions to our problems, but we don't always find them.
4. We need to _____ this problem thoroughly before we decide on a solution.
5. It seems like my best ideas always _____ me in the middle of the night.
6. Who do you _____ when you're trying to solve a problem?
7. They wanted to redesign the office but _____ the same level of comfort.
8. There is often a way that we can _____ other's experiences to our own. Then we can learn from them and apply this knowledge to our own lives.

## 2 GRAMMAR  *Likely* and *certain* + infinitive

Use *likely* or *certain* with an infinitive to talk about degrees of probability.

|  | Be (not) | Likely / certain | Infinitive |  |
|---|---|---|---|---|
| You | are | certain | to face | problems at work occasionally. |
|  | are (not) | likely | to solve | your problems by studying nature. |

**Notes**
- *Likely* is often used with *more* or *less*:
  *If you study hard, you are more likely to pass the test.*
  *Employees who don't have a mentor are less likely to succeed.*
- We often soften *certain* with *almost*:
  *The blue team is almost certain to win this game.*

>> FOR PRACTICE, GO TO PAGE 151

# 3 LISTENING

David Cruz | TSW Global Speaker Program
**Unit 9: Inspired by Nature**

**A** ▶09-14 Listen or watch. How was Eiji Nakatsu inspired by nature?

**B** ▶09-15 Read the Listening Skill. Listen or watch again. What verb does the speaker use instead of the underlined phrasal verb?

1. There's a reason that employers <u>care about</u> problem-solving skills!
2. Today I'm going to <u>talk about</u> one of those people and how nature helped him solve a problem.
3. You may <u>look for</u> inspiration in what other people have done or written about.

> **LISTENING SKILL Listen for tone and intended audience**
>
> Speakers use a different tone, or level of formality, depending on the audience they're speaking to. For example, in a formal educational talk, they may choose formal verbs instead of phrasal verbs, such as *discover* instead of *find out*. Listening for formal word choices can help you identify a speaker's tone.

**C** ▶09-16 Listen or watch again. Answer the questions.

1. What problem did Eiji Nakatsu need to solve?
   _____
2. Why was Eiji Nakatsu interested in the kingfisher?
   _____
3. What was the unexpected benefit of the new design?
   _____
4. Besides studying nature, how else do people look for inspiration?
   _____

**D** VOCABULARY EXPANSION Read each sentence from the talk. What do the underlined expressions mean?

1. <u>In the end</u>, the new trains were designed with a nose that looked very much like a kingfisher's bill.
   _____
2. There are robots that walk like spiders, a swimsuit <u>based on</u> the skin of a shark, and a paint that doesn't get dirty.
   _____
3. This kind of engineering is known as *biomimicry*, with the idea being that we can find solutions to human problems by studying, and <u>mimicking</u>, how nature has solved them.
   _____

**E** PAIRS Compare answers in 3D.

# 4 DISCUSSION

**A** THINK When did you last have a problem at work, school, or home? Take notes.

| What was your problem? | How did you solve it? |
| --- | --- |
|  |  |

**B** PAIRS Share your problems and solutions.

**C** CATEGORIZE How many people asked someone for help? How many read or watched something? How many solved the problem another way?

■ I CAN DISCUSS WAYS TO SOLVE PROBLEMS.

## HANA LEE
@HanaL

How many times do you think you'll change jobs in your lifetime? Read this article for some interesting stats.

## 1 BEFORE YOU READ

**A** PAIRS Have you ever had to look for a job? What was your experience like?

**B** ▶09-17 VOCABULARY Listen. Then listen and repeat. Do you know these words?

| realistic | satisfying | a requirement | a salary | a quality | open-minded |

**>> FOR DEFINITIONS AND PRACTICE, GO TO PAGE 151**

## 2 READ

**A** PREVIEW Read the title. Look at the photo and the lists of questions. What do you think the article will be about?

**B** ▶09-18 Read and listen to the article. Was your prediction correct?

# What Kind of Job Is Best for You?

You're ready to look for your first job, or maybe you're ready to change careers. Unless you're one of those unique people who has always known what you've wanted to do, you may be confused
5 about how to choose and get the job you really want. Since most people spend about 35% of their lives working, this is an extremely important thing to learn how to do.

Start by asking yourself a basic question:

10 *If money were not an issue, what job would I really want to do?*

Of course, it's not always possible to do exactly what you want. For example, it may not be realistic for you to suddenly become an astronaut or a
15 professional soccer coach. However, if you can figure out what interests, beliefs, needs, and skills you have, you'll have a better chance of finding a job you love.

There are many tools that can help you do this, such as
20 online career tests. But you can easily decide on your own what job is going to be the most interesting and satisfying for you by asking yourself these questions:

- What interests me the most?
- What beliefs and values are the most important to me?
25 - What are my personal requirements about salary, location, and level of challenge?

In other words, ask yourself what job will make you want to get out of bed every day, excited to go to work.

Now that you've identified the kind of job you want, let's
30 look at the best ways to see if you are a good match for this job by focusing on your abilities rather than job titles. Consider the following questions:

- What do I really do well?
- What skills do I like using?
35 - What other qualities can I bring to a job?

>>

Once you've determined what job is right for you, there are some basic things you can do to make sure you get hired.

- Research the company you're applying to.
40 - Find out everything you can about the position.
- Prepare yourself for answering interview questions and selling yourself.

Even if you don't find the perfect job right away, don't worry. Nowadays people change jobs an average of 45 twelve times in their lifetime. With the experience you've gained from your first attempt, you're more likely to have a better chance of finding the right job for you the next time. Also, as you decide which job is best for you, always remember to stay open-minded. You may 50 even find something you like that you never expected.

## 3 CHECK YOUR UNDERSTANDING

**A** Read the article again. What is the main idea?

**B** Answer the questions, according to the article.

1. Why is it important to start by asking yourself what you really want to do?

   _____

2. What should you focus on instead of job titles?

   _____

3. What can you do to get hired after you figure out what kind of job you want?

   _____

4. Why shouldn't you worry if you don't find your perfect job right away?

   _____

**C** CLOSE READING  Reread lines 1–8 in the article. Then circle the correct answers.

1. In line 3, the writer calls some people *unique* because it is unusual for people to ___ .
   a. change careers when they are older
   b. start working when they are very young
   c. choose a career when they are very young

2. In line 7, the word *this* refers to ___ .
   a. choosing and getting a job you want
   b. spending 35% of your life working
   c. knowing when to start a new career

**D** Read the Reading Skill. Then reread the article. Find and underline the different ways the writer describes the idea of a "dream job."

**E** PAIRS  What is the article about? Retell the most important ideas. Use your own words.

> **READING SKILL** Emphasize ideas
>
> Writers often write the same things in different ways to emphasize ideas. Doing this also helps to keep a text interesting and avoid repetition.

What is the most common dream job in the world? 🔍

## 4 MAKE IT PERSONAL

**A** THINK  What is your dream job? Do you think this article will help you find it? What other things could you do?

**B** PAIRS  Share your ideas. Are your dream jobs realistic? How could you find them?

▢ I CAN READ ABOUT FINDING A JOB.

**HANA LEE**

@HanaL

Just received this letter of recommendation from my boss. So touched by what he wrote.

## 1 BEFORE YOU WRITE

**A**   What do people usually need letters of recommendation for?

**B**   Complete the sentences with the words in the box.

| hesitate     dedicated     asset |
| --- |

1. If you notice a problem, don't _____ to call me. I want to know right away.
2. Frank's knowledge of food was a real _____ to us when we were planning our restaurant menu.
3. Sarah remained _____ to her charity work. She never missed a day all year.

**C**   Read the letter of recommendation. Why was it written?

> Dear Director of Admissions:
>
> It is my pleasure to recommend Hana Lee for the MBA program at the International University of Business. Hana has been a sales and marketing representative at TSW for three years, and she is a valuable member of my team.
>
> One of Hana's best qualities is her ability to communicate with others. Last year, she ran a seminar at our local office to explain some of the new company rules and regulations. Her presentation was so good that it was filmed and used for training purposes at TSW offices around the world.
>
> In addition, Hana has always been extremely dedicated to her work. Last month, we had a very short time to complete an extremely important project for our main sales and marketing office. Hana stayed late every day and put in extra hours during the weekend to make sure that the project was completed on time.
>
> Furthermore, Hana demonstrates an exceptional ability to take on leadership roles. Two weeks ago, we needed someone to create a new marketing strategy for one of our most important clients. Hana volunteered to be in charge and put together a team of ten people. Because of Hana's hard work, the team finished the project on time, and it was a huge success.
>
> In conclusion, I believe that Hana is an exceptional candidate for the MBA program at your university. I am certain that her talent, experience, and personality will help her to excel and make her an asset to the program.
>
> If you would like any additional information about Hana, please don't hesitate to contact me.
>
> Sincerely,
>
> John Park
> Human Resources Coordinator

**D** Read the letter of recommendation again. Complete the chart.

| Reason for the letter of recommendation | |
|---|---|
| | |

| | Hana's strengths | Examples of these strengths |
|---|---|---|
| 1 | | |
| 2 | | |
| 3 | | |

| Restatement of the reason for the letter of recommendation |
|---|
| |

## 2 FOCUS ON WRITING

Read the Writing Skill. Then reread the letter of recommendation. Underline the words and phrases that are used to add information.

> **WRITING SKILL** Use transition words and phrases to add information
>
> Add information by using words and phrases such as *in addition, moreover, furthermore, also, besides,* and *what's more.*

## 3 PLAN YOUR WRITING

**A** THINK Imagine that you are writing a letter of recommendation for someone. Who are you writing it for? Why are you writing it? What are the person's strengths? Draw a chart like the one in 1D.

**B** PAIRS Talk about the person you are recommending and what you are recommending this person for. Explain the person's strengths.

## 4 WRITE

Write a letter of recommendation for someone. Use transition words and phrases to add information. Use the letter of recommendation in 1C as a model.

> **Pre-writing tip**
> Ask the person you are writing the letter of recommendation for if anything special should be included. This will help you with the brainstorming process.

## 5 REVISE YOUR WRITING

**A** PAIRS Exchange letters of recommendation and read each other's writing.

1. Did your partner clearly explain his or her reason for writing the recommendation?
2. Did your partner include the person's strengths?
3. Did your partner include specific examples of the person's strengths?
4. Did your partner use transition words and phrases to add information?

**B** PAIRS Can your partner improve his or her letter of recommendation? Make suggestions.

## 6 PROOFREAD

Read your letter of recommendation again. Check your

- spelling
- punctuation
- capitalization

☐ I CAN WRITE A LETTER OF RECOMMENDATION.

# PUT IT TOGETHER

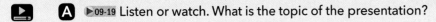

## 1 PRESENTATION PROJECT

▶ **A** ▶09-19 Listen or watch. What is the topic of the presentation?

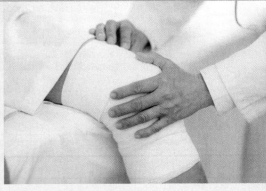

▶ **B** ▶09-20 Listen or watch again. Answer the questions.

1. What job does Junio want?

   _____

2. Why did Junio get interested in this type of work?

   _____

3. What qualifications does Junio have?

   _____

**C** Read the presentation skill. Is this something you knew already?

**D** Make your own presentation.

> **PRESENTATION SKILL**
>
> **Ignore distractions**
> When you are giving your presentation, do not get bothered by other noises or distractions in the room. Stay focused on what you have to say.

Step 1 When people prepare for an interview, they often think of an "elevator speech," which is a clear and simple way to respond when an interviewer says, "Tell us about yourself." The typical response is a short description of the person's background, qualities, and strengths. Pretend that you are preparing an elevator speech for your dream job.

Step 2 Prepare a two-minute presentation with your elevator speech. Bring an item or picture that is related to your dream job.

Step 3 Give your presentation to the class. Remember to use the presentation skill. Answer questions and get feedback.

> How did you do? Complete the self-evaluation on page 165.

## 2 REFLECT AND PLAN

**A** Look back through the unit. Check (✓) the things you learned. Highlight the things you need to learn.

**Speaking objectives**
- ☐ Ask for help and show appreciation
- ☐ Talk about possible changes at work
- ☐ Discuss ways to solve problems

**Vocabulary**
- ☐ Elements of the writing process
- ☐ Employment terms

**Conversation**
- ☐ Express appreciation

**Pronunciation**
- ☐ Intonation in lists

**Listening**
- ☐ Listen for tone and intended audience

**Grammar**
- ☐ *Would / Do you mind* for permission and requests
- ☐ Modals with the passive
- ☐ *Likely* and *certain* + infinitive

**Reading**
- ☐ Emphasize ideas

**Writing**
- ☐ Use transition words and phrases to add information

**B** What will you do to learn the things you highlighted? For example, use your app, review your Student Book, or do other practice. Make a plan.

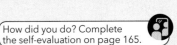

> ‹ Notes            Done
>
> In the app, do the Lesson 1 Vocabulary activities: Elements of the writing process.

# 10 HAS THE CITY CHANGED?

## LEARNING GOALS

In this unit, you
- ⊘ talk about how cities change
- ⊘ talk about getting around a city
- ⊘ discuss lost and found items
- ⊘ read about how a city has improved
- ⊘ write about a favorite place

## GET STARTED

**A** Read the unit title and learning goals.

**B** Look at the photo. What do you see?

**C** Now read Oscar's message. How does he feel about cities?

**OSCAR BLANCO**
@OscarB

I never get tired of going back to cities I love. It's like visiting old friends.

113

## 1 VOCABULARY
City features and changes

### OSCAR BLANCO
@OscarB

Almost didn't recognize parts of San Diego. So much has changed since my last visit.

**A** ▶10-01 **Listen. Then listen and repeat.**

**City features**

**a fountain:** an object that makes water go into the air, used as a decoration outside

**a landmark:** something that is easy to recognize and helps you know where you are

**an amphitheater:** a large theater with no roof and rows of seats in a half-circle

**a waterfront:** a part of a town or an area of land next to a lake, a river, or an ocean

**a plaza:** a public area or marketplace surrounded by buildings

**City changes**

**tear down:** to destroy or knock down a building

**redevelop:** to make an area more modern by adding new buildings or improving old ones

**renovate:** to repair and paint something, especially a building, so that it looks new

**construct:** to build something large, such as a building or bridge

**B** Label the pictures with words from 1A.

1. _____   2. _____   4. _____   6. _____   8. _____

3. _____   5. _____   7. _____

**C** PAIRS Think about an area you know that needs to be improved. Discuss what you would do and explain why. Use words from 1A.

## 2 GRAMMAR  *Do* or *did* for emphasis

We can use *do* or *did* in affirmative statements to show that we feel strongly about something.

| Subject | *Do / did* | Base form of the verb | |
|---------|-----------|----------------------|---|
| I | do | like | the new fountain. |
| We | did | go | to Horton Plaza Park. |

Notes
* We can use *do / did* to express a contrast: *I didn't go to the beach, but I did visit the plaza.*
* We can also use *do / did* to make a correction:
  **A:** *I heard you didn't like the performance.*   **B:** *No, I did like it. The singers were amazing!*

**>> FOR PRACTICE, GO TO PAGE 152**

# 3 PRONUNCIATION

**A** ▶10-02 Read and listen to the pronunciation note.

**B** ▶10-03 Listen. Notice the emphasis of *do, does,* and *did.* Then listen and repeat.

> **Emphasis of *do, does, did***
>
> When *do, does,* or *did* are used to emphasize, correct, or contrast, they are pronounced with extra length and loudness. For example: *I haven't been here long, but I DID notice a lot of new parks.*

1. A: Do you have time to go down to the waterfront for lunch?
   B: No, not today. But I do have time to go to the new outdoor market. It's pretty close.
2. A: That new office building downtown is so ugly.
   B: I know! But it does have solar roof panels, so it's environmentally friendly!
3. A: The new open areas downtown look fantastic.
   B: I think so, too. But it did mean a lot of apartment buildings were torn down.

**C** PAIRS Practice the conversations in 3B. Then create your own conversation, using *do, does,* and *did* for emphasis.

# 4 CONVERSATION

**A** ▶10-04 Listen or watch. What do Pablo and Oscar talk about?

**B** ▶10-05 Listen or watch again. Answer the questions.
1. Where has Oscar just flown in from?
2. Why did Pablo use to go there a lot?
3. What is the city building along the waterfront?
4. Why is Pablo concerned about the new buildings?

 Do you think Pablo will check out Horton Plaza Park the next time he's in San Diego?

**C** ▶10-06 FOCUS ON LANGUAGE Listen or watch. Complete the conversation.

> Pablo: Did you have a chance to see the city?
>
> Oscar: A little. I was pretty busy meeting with clients during the day, but I _____ go out one night after work. I saw a free concert in Horton Plaza Park.
>
> Pablo: Horton Plaza Park? That's downtown, right?
>
> Oscar: Yeah, they _____ that whole area. They restored the old _____ and built a wonderful new amphitheater.
>
> Pablo: Nice!

# 5 TRY IT YOURSELF

**A** THINK What city do you know well? What changes or improvements have been made to it over the years? Take notes.

**B** PAIRS Share your ideas. What are some of the changes you really like or dislike? Use the conversation in 4C as an example.

**C** COMPARE Talk about the cities as a class. What are some of the most common changes and improvements? Which city has changed the most?

■ I CAN TALK ABOUT HOW CITIES CHANGE.

## OSCAR BLANCO
@OscarB

Back in NY. You won't believe what happened to me on my way to work this morning.

 **1 VOCABULARY** Verbs for getting around

**A** ▶10-07 Listen. Then listen and repeat.

| | |
|---|---|
| **rush:** to move or do something quickly because you do not have much time | **pull out of:** to drive a car out of a place where it is parked |
| **head out:** to leave in a particular direction | **pull over:** to drive to the side of the road and stop |
| **get off:** to leave a bus, plane, or train | **be stuck:** to not be able to move |
| **get on:** to enter a bus, plane, or train | |
| **pull into:** to drive a car into a place to park | |

**B** Label the pictures with words from 1A.

1. _____

3. _____

5. _____

2. _____

4. _____

6. _____

**C** PAIRS Explain how you get to school or work. Use words from 1A.

## 2 GRAMMAR Past perfect with adverbial clauses of time: Review and expand

We can use adverbial clauses of time to show when something in the past happened in relation to another event in the past. Adverbial clauses of time are introduced by time expressions such as *as soon as*, *when*, *before*, *by the time*, *after*, and *once*.

| Adverbial clause of time | | | Main clause | | |
|---|---|---|---|---|---|
| **Time expression** | **Simple past** | | | **Past perfect** | |
| By the time | I arrived | at my friend's house, | everyone | had gone | home. |
| **Time expression** | **Past perfect** | | | **Simple past** | |
| After | I had passed | a few stations, | I | knew | something wasn't right. |

**Notes**
- Adverbial clauses are dependent clauses and cannot stand alone as a sentence.
- When an adverbial clause of time begins a sentence, use a comma to separate the clauses.
- Do not use a comma to separate the clauses when the adverbial clause of time comes after the independent clause.

**>> FOR PRACTICE, GO TO PAGE 153**

# 3 CONVERSATION SKILL

**A** ▶10-08 Read the conversation skill. Listen to the conversations. Notice how one speaker introduces a popular opinion.

> **Introduce a popular opinion**
>
> We can introduce opinions that a lot of people share by saying things like:
> *Everyone says that…*
> *It's a well-known fact that…*
> *Most people think that…*
> *I've heard from so many people that…*

1. **A:** Look how bad the traffic is today.
   **B:** Yeah, it's terrible. Everyone says that it gets worse this time of year.
2. **A:** I couldn't catch a cab this morning.
   **B:** Tell me about it. I've heard from so many people that it's faster to just take the bus.

**B** ▶10-09 Listen and complete the conversations.

1. **A:** The subway system here is fantastic! The trains are clean and they're always on time.
   **B:** Yep! _____ this city has the best subway system in the world.
2. **A:** I tried to take the new bridge this morning, but I got stuck in traffic for an hour.
   **B:** Oh. I'm sorry to hear that. _____ it's faster to take the old bridge.

**C** PAIRS Practice the conversations in 3A and 3B.

# 4 CONVERSATION

**A** ▶10-10 Listen or watch. What do Oscar and Pablo mainly talk about?

**B** ▶10-11 Listen or watch again. Answer the questions.

1. Why was Oscar late for his first meeting?
2. What transportation problem did Pablo have last winter?
3. What had happened by the time Pablo arrived at his friend's house?
4. How could Pablo's problem with getting around have been worse?

> Do you think Oscar will make it to his meeting on time? Why or why not?

**C** ▶10-12 FOCUS ON LANGUAGE Listen or watch. Complete the conversation.

**Oscar:** _____ I had passed a few stations, I knew something wasn't right. So I _____ at the next stop, but then I couldn't cross over to the other platform.

**Pablo:** Ugh.

**Oscar:** I had to leave the station and cross the street. Of course, it took forever for the light to change.

**Pablo:** That's awful, but don't feel too bad. I've lived here for years, and I still have trouble with public transportation from time to time.

**Oscar:** Yeah, _____ this isn't the easiest city to get around in.

# 5 TRY IT YOURSELF

**A** THINK Remember when you had a difficult time getting around somewhere. What happened? Take notes.

**B** PAIRS Share your experiences. Use the conversation in 4C as an example.

**C** REPORT Tell the class about your partner's experience. Who had the most interesting experience? Whose experience was the worst?

■ I CAN TALK ABOUT GETTING AROUND A CITY.

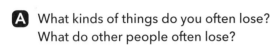

# LESSON 3  DISCUSS LOST AND FOUND ITEMS

**OSCAR BLANCO**
@OscarB

Just watched a talk about lost and found items. I never realized how much stuff people leave on trains and buses!

## 1 BEFORE YOU LISTEN

**A** What kinds of things do you often lose? What do other people often lose?

**B** ▶10-13 VOCABULARY  Listen. Then listen and repeat.

> **an exhibition:** a public show of something such as art
> **wander:** to walk slowly around without having a clear idea of where you want to go
> **random:** chosen without any pattern
> **mass transit:** a system of trains or buses that people use to travel around an area
> **on display:** in a public place for people to see
> **reunite:** to bring people or things together after they have been separated
> **belongings:** things that you own, especially the ones that you carry with you
> **thrilled:** very excited, pleased, or happy
> **recover:** to get back something that was lost or stolen

**C** Complete the sentences with words from 1B.

1. I was _____ to find my wallet after I thought I had lost it.
2. Millions of people ride _____ in this city.
3. We saw an interesting _____ of black-and-white photographs.
4. We're going to _____ around until we see someplace interesting to stop.
5. After six years of living in different countries, he was finally able to _____ with his brother.
6. We saw her paintings _____ at a café downtown.
7. He was hoping to _____ his bicycle after it was stolen, but he never did.
8. Make sure you have all of your _____ before you get off the train.
9. The art director picked _____ photos to put on the museum's website. No one knew which pictures she was going to choose.

## 2 GRAMMAR  Non-restrictive relative clauses for comments

Use non-restrictive relative clauses to make a comment about a main clause. These relative clauses always begin with *which*. They refer to the entire main clause.

| Main clause | Relative clause | |
|---|---|---|
| | *Which* | |
| A lot of these items are never picked up, | which | isn't surprising. |
| It will give me a reason to visit the office, | which | could be interesting. |

**Note:** These clauses are more common in informal speech than in writing:
A: *What are you still doing here?*
B: *They said I have to wait another hour, which is ridiculous!*

**>> FOR PRACTICE, GO TO PAGE 154**

## 3 LISTENING

**A** ▶10-14 Listen or watch. What was in the *Lost Collection*?

**B** ▶10-15 Read the Listening Skill. Then listen or watch again. Complete the sentences with the words used by the speaker. Then check (✓) the correct box to show whether the words show a positive or negative attitude.

TSW MEDIA

Adriana Lopez I TSW Global Speaker Program
**Unit 10: Lost and Found**

| | Positive | Negative |
|---|---|---|
| 1. The exhibition title, *The Lost Collection*, _____ to me. | ☐ | ☐ |
| 2. Richard Walker had a(n) _____ idea. | ☐ | ☐ |
| 3. You can imagine his _____ at recovering his lost art. | ☐ | ☐ |

**C** ▶10-16 Listen or watch again. Answer the questions.

1. What is the London Transport lost property office?
   _____

2. What happens to items that are never picked up from the lost property office?
   _____

3. What was Richard Walker's idea?
   _____

4. Why was one man very excited to find his portrait?
   _____

> **LISTENING SKILL  Listen for attitude**
>
> Speakers show how they feel about a topic by choosing words that sound positive or negative. They may show a positive attitude by using adjectives like *wonderful*, nouns like *happiness*, or verbs like *enjoy*.
>
> They may show a negative attitude with adjectives like *difficult*, nouns like *failure*, or verbs like *dislike*.

**D** VOCABULARY EXPANSION  Read each sentence from the talk. What do the underlined expressions mean?

1. I just happened to be near an art gallery with some <u>time to kill</u>. I noticed this interesting black-and-white painting in the window.
   _____

2. Inside I found a rather random collection of artwork—paintings of trees and flowers, <u>portraits</u> of children, photographs of laughing friends.
   _____

3. If you ever lose something on a train, on a bus, or anywhere at all, maybe you'll make an effort to <u>track it down</u>.
   _____

**E** PAIRS  Compare answers in 3D.

## 4 DISCUSSION

**A** THINK  When did you lose or find something interesting or valuable? Complete the chart.

| What was the item? | |
|---|---|
| How / where did you lose or find it? | |
| If you lost it, did you find it? How? | |
| If you found it, what did you do with it? | |

**B** DISCUSS  In small groups, share your stories. Include comments about how you felt.

**C** COMPARE  Share your stories with the class. How many people lost or found something really valuable? How many people were reunited with lost items?

☐ I CAN DISCUSS LOST AND FOUND ITEMS.

**OSCAR BLANCO**
@OscarB

How did a densely populated, urban island become the greenest city on the planet?

## 1 BEFORE YOU READ

**A**   **PAIRS**   Think about where you live or a city nearby. How green is it? What could be done to make it greener?

**B**   ▶10-17 **VOCABULARY**   Listen. Then listen and repeat. Do you know these words?

> lush    greenery    eco-friendly    a structure    a commitment    sustain
> an impression    paradise
>
> **>> FOR DEFINITIONS AND PRACTICE, GO TO PAGE 154**

## 2 READ

**A**   **PREVIEW**   Read the title and look at the pictures. What do you think the article will be about?

**B**   ▶10-18 Read and listen to the article. Was your prediction correct?

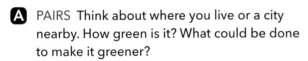

# THE GREENEST CITY IN ASIA

**Home**
Shopping
Travel
*reviews*
*news*
*guides*
*blogs*
*articles*

Singapore was the last stop on the tour my editor sent me on to find the greenest of the green cities in Asia. As soon as I got off the plane, I realized that Singapore isn't like any of the other cities I've ever visited. To begin with, it's both a big city and a small country. Its approximately six million residents are packed into only 720 square kilometers (280 square miles) of land. Yet,
5   compared to other cities with similar populations, it didn't feel crowded at all. Why? Possibly because there are so many parks, grassy spaces, trees, and gardens, which give it the feeling of having open space everywhere.

When I first got this assignment, I decided to learn how Singapore has become so green. In my research, I found photos of Singapore in the 1950s, when it looked just like any other crowded
10   city. On May 11, 1967, however, Singapore's first prime minister, Lee Kuan Yew, introduced his vision of Singapore becoming a "City in a Garden." He planned to redevelop Singapore into a well-organized city with lush greenery and clean air. Now, many years later, Singapore has millions of trees, hundreds of parks, and rules about how buildings must be eco-friendly.

The first stop on my tour of Singapore was the amazing Gardens by the Bay, a 250-acre nature
15   park with three waterfront gardens located in the middle of the city. It includes the famous Supertree Grove, featuring huge tree-like structures that are covered with tens of thousands of plants and collect enough solar energy to run a nightly lightshow.

My next stop, the Pinnacle@Duxton, is a public housing complex constructed in 2009 as part of former Prime Minister Lee's plan to
20   make the city more attractive and environmentally friendly. Its seven 50-story buildings are all connected at the 26th and 50th floors by sky bridges that have the world's longest sky gardens. On the 50th-floor sky bridge, residents and visitors can relax, exercise, and enjoy amazing views surrounded by nature.

25   Last, I headed out to the central business district to see the Parkroyal on Pickering Hotel, which is one of the best examples of Singapore's commitment to the environment. This hotel is covered with trees, plants, and gardens that are sustained by solar power and recycled rainwater. There are also waterfalls that provide a
30   natural cooling system and great places to relax.

**Supertree Grove in Gardens by the Bay**

**Parkroyal on Pickering Hotel**

> By the time I left Singapore, I felt like I had accomplished my goal—to find the greenest of the green cities in Asia. My overall impression was that Singapore was not just a "City in a
35 Garden." It was also a "Paradise in a Garden."

Now, I can't wait to go back to Singapore someday. I'm sure that when I'm there, I'll discover new ways that it is keeping former Prime Minister Lee's eco-friendly vision alive.

Pinnacle@Duxton

## 3 CHECK YOUR UNDERSTANDING

**A** Read the article again. What is the main idea?

**B** According to what you read in the article, answer the following questions.

1. How did Lee Kuan Yew plan to make Singapore into a "City in a Garden"?

   _____

2. What three places did the writer visit on his tour of Singapore?

   _____

3. How have these places made Singapore a greener city?

   _____

4. Why does the writer think that Singapore will keep Lee's vision alive?

   _____

**C** CLOSE READING  Reread lines 2–7 in the article. Then circle the correct answers.

1. In line 4, the writer uses *Yet* to show that Singapore is ___ .
   a. the same as other large cities
   b. different from other large cities
   c. more crowded than other large cities

2. In line 6, *it* refers to ___ .
   a. Singapore
   b. open space
   c. the feeling

**D** Read the Reading Skill. Then circle the correct answer.

1. Reread lines 1–3. What can you infer about the writer?
   a. He has not flown on a plane before.
   b. He has visited other big cities before.
   c. Singapore is the first big city he's visited.

2. Reread lines 8–13. What can you infer about the writer?
   a. He was not an expert on Singapore's redevelopment before he was told to go there.
   b. He was an expert on Singapore's redevelopment before he was told to go there.
   c. He does not think that it is important to do research before writing a story.

> **READING SKILL Make inferences**
>
> As you read, use information from the text and your own knowledge to make educated guesses about what the writer does not say directly.

**E** PAIRS  What is the article about? Retell the most important ideas. Use your own words.

## 4 MAKE IT PERSONAL

> What are cities around you doing to become greener? 🔍

**A** THINK  What else can cities do to become more eco-friendly? Make a list.

**B** PAIRS  Share your ideas. Choose the three best ways that cities could become more eco-friendly.

■ I CAN READ ABOUT HOW A CITY HAS IMPROVED.

**OSCAR BLANCO**
@OscarB

Have you ever returned to one of your favorite places and noticed it has changed? How did you feel?

## 1 BEFORE YOU WRITE

**A** What is one of your favorite places to visit? What do you like about it?

**B** Complete the sentences with the words in the box.

| browse | trendy |
| --- | --- |

1. The new store sells _____ clothes from around the world.
2. It's fun to _____ through the books, even if you aren't going to buy any of them.

**C** Read the blog. What is it about? Does it make you want to visit Chiang Mai?

Blog │ About │ Contact 　　　　　　　　　　　🔍 Search

# Chiang Mai, Then and Now

About
RSS Feed
Social Media
Recent Posts
Archives
Email

Chiang Mai is one of my favorite places in the world. I've been going to this small, beautiful city in northern Thailand for more than twenty years. Every time I'm there, I'm amazed by how much the city has changed and how much it has stayed the same.

On the one hand, so much of what I love about Chiang Mai has been the same for as long as I can remember. For example, I can still eat steaming hot pad Thai at one of the amazing street food stalls. Likewise, I can browse the traditional markets that have been selling goods for hundreds of years. The first time I visited Chiang Mai, I took tuk-tuks everywhere I wanted to go. These three-wheeled motorized taxis were there for me then, and they're still there for me now. Finally, whenever I'm in the city in late fall, I can always enjoy the Loi Krathong Festival and float a candle in a banana-leaf container down the Ping River.

On the other hand, a lot has changed in Chiang Mai over the years. When I first arrived in the city, I often ate lunch at a famous old restaurant that had been owned by the same family for generations. The last time I went back, however, the restaurant had been torn down and replaced with a convenience store. In the same way, some of the old shops I used to go to have been replaced with huge air-conditioned shopping malls offering the trendiest brands from around the world. Although I still like to take tuk-tuks, they aren't as popular as they used to be. Nowadays, most tourists and locals prefer to use the new ride-sharing services when they need to go somewhere.

While some people might be bothered by these changes, I'm excited to see the city adapt and grow. I can't wait to see what Chiang Mai will look like twenty years from now.

**Leave a Reply**

Enter your comment here…

**D** Read the blog again. Take notes in the chart.

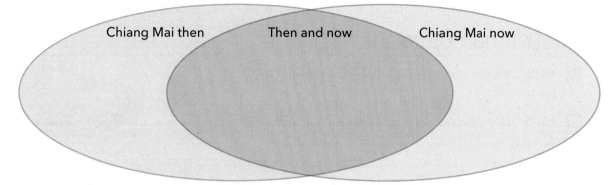

Chiang Mai then | Then and now | Chiang Mai now

## 2 FOCUS ON WRITING

Read the Writing Skill. Then reread the blog. Underline the words and phrases that are used to show comparison and contrast.

> **WRITING SKILL** Use a range of transition words to show comparison and contrast
>
> Words and phrases such as *similarly, likewise, in the same way*, and *in the same fashion* compare ideas. Words and phrases such as *but, however, on the other hand, while, although,* and *on the contrary* contrast ideas.

## 3 PLAN YOUR WRITING

**A** THINK What is one of your favorite places to go to? How has it changed? How has it stayed the same? Draw a chart like the one in 1D.

**B** PAIRS Talk about your favorite place to go to.

One of my favorite places to go to is Haeundae Beach in Busan, South Korea...

## 4 WRITE

Write a blog about how one of your favorite places has changed and stayed the same over the years. Use the blog in 1C as a model.

## 5 REVISE YOUR WRITING

**A** PAIRS Exchange blogs and read each other's writing.

1. Did your partner describe how the place has changed and stayed the same?
2. Did your partner use transition words to compare and contrast ideas?

> **Revising tip**
> Make your descriptions as strong and vivid as possible. Use a thesaurus to find the best words to describe things. Stronger, more vivid descriptions will make your writing more interesting.

**B** PAIRS Can your partner improve his or her blog? Make suggestions.

## 6 PROOFREAD

Read your blog again. Check your

- spelling
- punctuation
- capitalization

# PUT IT TOGETHER

## 1 PRESENTATION PROJECT

**A** ▶10-19 Listen or watch. What is the topic of the presentation?

**B** ▶10-20 Listen or watch again. Answer the questions.

1. Where is the statue of Stepan the Plumber?
   _____

2. How is the statue different from other statues?
   _____

3. Why does Misaki like it?
   _____

**C** Read the presentation skill. Why do you think this skill might be helpful?

**D** Make your own presentation.

**Step 1** Do research to find an example of art, such as a statue or mural, in a public place. Explain what the art is, where it is, and whether you like it or not.

**Step 2** Prepare a two-minute presentation about the public art you've chosen. Remember to use the presentation skill. Bring a photo of it.

**Step 3** Give your presentation to the class. Answer questions and get feedback.

> **PRESENTATION SKILL**
>
> **Explain terms that may be new to the audience**
> When you are preparing your presentation, think about vocabulary that you might need to define or explain to your audience members.

How did you do? Complete the self-evaluation on page 165.

## 2 REFLECT AND PLAN

**A** Look back through the unit. Check (✓) the things you learned. Highlight the things you need to learn.

**Speaking objectives**
- ☐ Talk about cities and how they change
- ☐ Talk about getting around a city
- ☐ Discuss lost and found items

**Vocabulary**
- ☐ City features and changes
- ☐ Verbs for getting around

**Conversation**
- ☐ Introduce a popular opinion

**Pronunciation**
- ☐ Emphasis of *do, does, did*

**Listening**
- ☐ Listen for attitude

**Grammar**
- ☐ *Do* or *did* for emphasis
- ☐ Past perfect with adverbial clauses of time
- ☐ Non-restrictive relative clauses for comments

**Reading**
- ☐ Make inferences

**Writing**
- ☐ Use a range of transition words and phrases to show comparison and contrast

**B** What will you do to learn the things you highlighted? For example, use your app, review your Student Book, or do other practice. Make a plan.

Review the Conversation Skill: Introduce a popular opinion, page 117.

**A** Complete the interview. Use the correct form of the present perfect continuous.

**Interviewer:** Thank you very much for joining me today.

**Jessica Star:** It's my pleasure! <u>I've been filming</u> a new movie for the
**1 (I / film)**
past two months, so this is actually a nice break.

**I:** It sounds like you've been busy! What _____ on lately?
**2 (you / work)**

**JS:** Well, _____ much sleep recently! _____ a
**3 (I / not get)**                  **4 (I / shoot)**
heartwarming new movie called *The Last Love*. It's about a
young girl who gets very sick, falls in love, and…you have to
watch it to know more!

**I:** I can't wait to see it!

**JS:** You're also in luck because _____ to share a little surprise with everyone
**5 (we / plan)**
today! I recently recorded my first single, and you will be able to hear it in the new
movie! _____ about getting into singing for the past few years, and I'm really
**6 (I / think)**
happy to finally get started on this new adventure.

**I:** Wow! That's so exciting! What helped you make this decision?

**JS:** My parents have always supported me, but recently _____ me to focus more
**7 (they / encourage)**
on my singing. It was their support that helped me take this new step.

**I:** That's wonderful! I love hearing stories like yours.

**B** Read about Matt Rock's new album. Circle the correct form of the verbs.

## Popstar News!   MATT ROCK RECORDS NEW ALBUM!

Matt Rock announced today that he **(1) has recently recorded /
has recently been recording** a new album with his band. He and his band
members **(2) have worked / have been working** on the album for several
months. They **(3) haven't finished / haven't been finishing** it yet, but they hope
it will come out next year. In an interview, Rock said that he **(4) has been waiting / has waited**
for weeks to share this news with his fans. Many news outlets **(5) have been talking /
have talked** about this surprising news for hours, and his fans **(6) have followed /
have been following** the whole story online with excitement. In the interview, Rock said that the
band **(7) has been trying / has tried** to make a new album for many years, and he hopes fans
are going to be happy with the album when it's released.

**C** MAKE IT PERSONAL Write sentences about what you have or haven't been doing
*recently / lately* using the present perfect continuous.

1. <u>I've been listening to some new music recently.</u>
2. _____
3. _____
4. _____

**A** Rewrite the sentences using *what* clauses for emphasis.

1. I was amazed by the soundtrack.
   <u>What amazed me was the soundtrack.</u>

2. He loved the cinematography.
   _____

3. John and Jason were scared by the violent scene.
   _____

4. Sarah was surprised by the narrator's voice.
   _____

5. Jeff hated the silly dialog.
   _____

6. She was bored by the predictable story.
   _____

7. My friends and I dislike the soundtrack the most.
   _____

**B** Complete the sentences with a word from each box.

| Ways to describe movies or TV shows | Elements of a movie or TV show |
|---|---|
| disliked   amazed   surprised   loved<br>~~liked~~   bored   upset | ending   setting   cinematography<br>narrator   soundtrack   plot   ~~dialog~~ |

1. The conversations between the characters were great! I can't believe how natural they sounded.
   What Jack _____liked_____ was the _____dialog_____ .

2. I couldn't get into the story. I kept checking my watch to see when it would be over.
   What _____ Rachel was the _____ .

3. I couldn't believe that the story took place in Philadelphia. That's where I grew up!
   What _____ Jenny was the _____ .

4. The music was the best part of the movie. I can't stop singing the songs.
   What Lena _____ was the _____ .

5. I cried when the hero died in the final scene. I really wanted him to survive.
   What _____ Brianna was the _____ .

6. The guy who described everything wasn't very good. His jokes weren't funny.
   What Ryan _____ was the _____ .

7. The images of the rainforest were incredible. I've never seen anything so beautiful.
   What _____ Ron was the _____ .

**C** MAKE IT PERSONAL  Think about your favorite movie, TV show, or book. Describe it using *what* clauses for emphasis and the prompts.

1. (amaze)    <u>What amazed me was the acting. The main character was great!</u>
2. (like)     _____
3. (surprise) _____
4. (dislike)  _____

**A** Complete the conversations with *by* and the correct form of the verb in the box.

| inspire   engage   listen   use   watch   ~~take~~ |
|---|

1. **A:** You know a lot about old movies! Did you learn about them ____ by taking ____ a class?
   **B:** No. I learned about them _____ lots and lots of old movies!
2. **A:** I love going to the movies. Have you been to the new movie theater?
   **B:** No, I haven't. I usually see the latest movies _____ a streaming service at home.
3. **A:** The dialog sounded so natural in that movie.
   **B:** Apparently, the writer was able to make the dialog sound so natural _____ to regular people talking on the street.
4. **A:** Do you know what that movie is about?
   **B:** It's about a woman who helps a village _____ the people there to be kinder to one another.
5. **A:** I don't think he's a great director. Why do people like him?
   **B:** He's become well-known _____ the audience in trying to work out the story.

**B** MAKE IT PERSONAL  Write sentences about how you normally do the activities in the box. Use *by* and a gerund.

| ~~learn English~~   get the latest news   discover new music   learn about new technology |
|---|

1. I learn English by watching a lot of old movies.
2. _____
3. _____
4. _____

# UNIT 1, LESSON 4  VOCABULARY PRACTICE

Read the definitions. Then complete the sentences with the words.

> **a transition:** the process of changing from one situation to another
> **adapt:** to change because you are in a new situation
> **disastrous:** very bad
> **an extra:** an actor in a movie or TV show who does not say anything but is part of a crowd
> **virtual reality:** pictures and sounds that a computer produces to make you feel as if you are in a particular place
> **an impact:** the effect or influence that someone or something has

1. Some singers are able to make the _____ from the music industry to the film industry easily.
2. The director hired me to be a(n) _____ for the battle scene.
3. The movie *Jaws* had quite a(n) _____ in the summer of 1975. People stopped going to the beach.
4. Some movie actors find it hard to _____ to acting on a stage in front of a live audience.
5. My date last night was _____ . The movie was very dull, and I spilled my soda.
6. The _____ video game made me feel like I was in a different world.

**A** Circle the correct conjunction to complete each conversation.

1. Store assistant: I have a question. Can a customer return a dress that looks like it's been worn?

   Manager: The customer can return the dress (*providing that*)/ *unless* the customer has a receipt.

2. Store assistant: Can a customer return an item without a packing slip?

   Manager: Yes. *As long as* / *Unless* the customer has a receipt or another proof of purchase, we can provide a refund.

3. Customer: Can I return this item? I bought it two months ago.

   Manager: No. *Unless* / *Providing that* you have a receipt, this item cannot be returned.

4. Customer: I bought this item last week and it broke.

   Manager: *Providing* / *Unless* you have the receipt, I can give you a refund or order a replacement for you.

5. Store assistant: The customer didn't have a receipt.

   Manager: *As long as* / *Unless* the customer can prove that she purchased the item here, we cannot give her a refund or store credit.

6. Store assistant: Can the customer return this other item?

   Manager: *Providing* / *Unless* the item is in its original packaging, the customer can return it.

7. Store assistant: What if the customer bought it two months ago?

   Manager: *As long as* / *Unless* the customer returns an item within thirty days, we can't give a full refund. We can only give store credit.

**B** Combine the two sentences using the conjunction in parentheses. Use commas where necessary. Do not change the order of the sentences.

1. You purchased this dress fewer than thirty days ago. You can't return it. (unless)
   Unless you purchased this dress fewer than thirty days ago, you can't return it.

2. You can get a full refund. The item is in its original packaging. (as long as)
   _____

3. A full refund is possible. You purchased this dress last week. (providing that)
   _____

4. You have a receipt. You cannot return this item. (unless)
   _____

5. It was already broken when you received it. They will replace it. (as long as)
   _____

6. It's still in new condition. They won't give me a refund. (unless)
   _____

7. You can return it. You pay a restocking fee. (providing that)
   _____

**C** MAKE IT PERSONAL Write sentences about the return policy of your favorite store. Use *as long as, providing (that),* and *unless.*

1. I can return things providing that I have a receipt.
2. _____
3. _____
4. _____

**A** Complete each sentence with the correct form of the verbs in parentheses.

1. If I had _____visited_____ a few more banks, I could __have gotten__ a better interest rate.
   (visit)                                                         (get)

2. If I had _____ out a loan, I could _____ a new car.
   (take out)                              (buy)

3. I might _____ a better deal if I had _____ .
   (get)                                   (shop around)

4. If I had _____ for the loan, I could _____ my own company.
   (qualify)                              (start)

5. I would _____ a house if the bank hadn't _____ my loan application.
   (purchase)                              (turn down)

6. If I had _____ my loan faster, I might _____ my credit score.
   (pay off)                              (improve)

7. I could _____ the roof on my house if the bank had _____ my loan.
   (fix)                                       (approve)

8. I could _____ a lower down payment if I had _____ more each month.
   (get)                                       (pay)

9. If I hadn't _____ so long to buy a car, I could _____ my car to the beach.
   (wait)                                       (drive)

**B** Combine the two sentences using the correct form of the past unreal conditional. Do not change the order of the sentences.

1. He didn't pay off the loan. They lowered his credit score.
   _If he had paid off the loan, they wouldn't have lowered his credit score._

2. He didn't improve his credit score. He got a high interest rate.
   _____

3. She didn't pay her bills on time. She got turned down for a loan.
   _____

4. They didn't shop around. They had to make a big down payment.
   _____

5. We didn't make a big down payment. We had to pay more each month.
   _____

6. I didn't save a lot of money last year. I had to take out a big loan.
   _____

7. He didn't pay off his first loan. He couldn't borrow more money.
   _____

8. We didn't do a lot of research. We couldn't get a great deal.
   _____

9. They didn't prepare their documents in time. They couldn't get approved for a loan.
   _____

**C** MAKE IT PERSONAL Write about things at home, school, or work you could have done to have gotten better results. Use the past unreal conditional.

1. _If I had gotten up earlier, I wouldn't have missed the train._
2. _____
3. _____
4. _____

# UNIT 2, LESSON 3 — CONNECTIVES TO EXPRESS CONTRAST AND SURPRISE

**A** Connect the sentences using the connectives in parentheses. Do not change the order of the sentences. Use a comma as needed.

1. My friends told me good things about the fundraiser. I found out later it was a scam. (however)
   My friends told me good things about the fundraiser. However, I found out later it was a scam.
2. The fundraising campaign video went viral. It has not helped raise much money. (even though)
   _____
3. On one hand, they want to make a donation to a charity for animals. They feel children's charities are more important. (on the other hand)
   _____
4. Taking out a loan is very common. Not everyone does it. (while)
   _____
5. The fundraising campaign started only this morning. We've already reached our goal. (however)
   _____
6. Emily can't find investors. She has a great business plan. (despite)
   _____

**B** MAKE IT PERSONAL What do you think about giving money to charity? Write sentences using connectives to show contrast or surprise.

1. I never give money to people collecting for charity on the street. However, a lot of my friends do.
2. _____
3. _____
4. _____

# UNIT 2, LESSON 4  VOCABULARY PRACTICE

Read the definitions. Then complete the sentences with the words.

> **a shelter:** a place where people can go if they have no home or are being treated badly
> **a mood:** the way you feel at a particular time
> **make a difference:** to do something that will have an important effect on someone or something
> **generous:** giving people more of your money or time than is expected
> **blood pressure:** the force with which blood moves through the body
> **a perspective:** a way of feeling about something that is influenced by the kind of person you are or by your experiences

1. When the charity met its fundraising goal, all the volunteers were in a good _____ .
2. The CEO recently made a(n) _____ offer to give everyone free computers.
3. Seeing how people in other parts of the world live has changed my _____ on life.
4. Reducing your stress can help you lower your _____ and feel better.
5. They stayed in a homeless _____ until they had enough money to buy a new home.
6. Volunteering is one way to _____ in other people's lives.

# UNIT 3, LESSON 1    GIVING AND ASKING FOR ADVICE

**A** Dan isn't feeling well. Give him advice by rewriting the sentences. Replace the underlined words with the words in parentheses.

1. He <u>should not</u> go to work tomorrow. (had better not)
   <u>He'd better not go to work tomorrow.</u>
2. He <u>should</u> rest. (ought to)
   _____
3. He <u>had better</u> drink plenty of fluids. (should)
   _____
4. He <u>had better not</u> take his medicine until after he eats. (should not)
   _____
5. He <u>should</u> put a cold, wet cloth on his head. (ought to)
   _____
6. He <u>should</u> visit his doctor if his symptoms get worse. (had better)
   _____
7. He <u>ought to</u> get a flu shot next year to avoid getting sick again. (should)
   _____

**B** Complete the conversations with the words in the box.

> had better not go    had better get    If I were you
> had better sit    should    ought    ~~should take~~

1. A: I've got a really bad headache.
   B: You __should take__ some pain medicine.
2. A: I have really bad muscle aches and pains.
   B: You _____ to lie down for a while.
3. A: I feel nauseous. What _____ I do?
   B: If I were you, I'd drink some ginger tea.
4. A: I'm really dizzy.
   B: You _____ down and eat something.
5. A: I feel really stuffed-up. What should I do?
   B: _____ , I'd take a hot shower.
6. A: I feel weak and extremely fatigued.
   B: You _____ lots of rest.
7. A: I think I have the flu.
   B: You _____ to work today.

**C** MAKE IT PERSONAL Your friend wants to avoid getting a cold. Give advice using the prompts.

1. (should)        <u>You should avoid going to crowded places.</u>
2. (had better)     _____
3. (ought to)       _____
4. (If I were you, I'd) _____

GRAMMAR PRACTICE    131

**A** Complete the conversations with the words in the box.

~~suggested~~ that elevating rest wearing me recommend

1. A: What did the doctor say?
   B: He ___suggested___ putting ice on three times a day.
2. A: What did the doctor _____ ?
   B: She recommended getting a cast.
3. A: What did the nurse tell you?
   B: She told _____ to wear a knee brace.
4. A: What did the doctor suggest?
   B: He suggested _____ a sling for my dislocated shoulder.
5. A: What did the nurse tell you?
   B: She told me to _____ my foot for a week.
6. A: What did the doctor recommend?
   B: She recommended _____ I use a neck brace.
7. A: What did the nurse suggest?
   B: She suggested _____ my foot.

**B** Complete the conversations with the words in parentheses. More than one answer may be possible.

1. A: What advice did the doctor give you about your fractured ankle?
   B: The doctor _____suggested (that) I wear_____ a cast.
   (suggested, wear)
2. A: What did the doctor say about your sprained wrist?
   B: The doctor _____ a wrist brace.
   (recommend, wear)
3. A: What did the doctor recommend doing about your dislocated shoulder?
   B: The doctor _____ a sling.
   (suggest, wear)
4. A: What did the doctor tell you to do about the muscle you pulled in your leg?
   B: The doctor _____ ice on it.
   (recommend, put)
5. A: What did the doctor suggest for walking around?
   B: The doctor _____ crutches.
   (tell, use)
6. A: What did the doctor say about your fractured arm?
   B: The doctor _____ a cast.
   (say, wear)

**C** MAKE IT PERSONAL What health advice have people given you recently? Write three sentences using reporting verbs.

1. _My friend suggested drinking apple cider vinegar._____
2. _____
3. _____
4. _____

**A** Combine the sentences using *not only…but also*.

1. The nurse gave her a bandage. The nurse gave her pain medicine.
   <u>The nurse gave her not only a bandage but also pain medicine.</u>

2. Karen injured her arm. Karen injured her shoulder.
   _____

3. Jeff has the flu. Jeff has a broken leg.
   _____

4. The doctor was impatient. The doctor was rude.
   _____

5. Medical equipment needs to be sterile. Medical equipment needs to be carefully organized.
   _____

6. Some microbes are harmless. Some microbes are good for our immune system.
   _____

**B** MAKE IT PERSONAL Write sentences about how you avoid getting sick and stay healthy. Use *not only… but also*.

1. <u>I avoid not only crowded places but also people who are sick.</u>
2. _____
3. _____
4. _____

# UNIT 3, LESSON 4  VOCABULARY PRACTICE

Read the definitions. Then complete the sentences with the words.

> **cancer:** a very serious disease in which cells in the body start to grow in an uncontrolled way
> **detect:** to notice or discover something, especially something that is not easy to see or hear
> **a seizure:** a short time when someone is unconscious and cannot control the movements of his or her body
> **a sensor:** something that is used to discover the presence of a scent or odor, light, heat, sound, movement, etc., especially in small amounts
> **identify:** to recognize and correctly name someone or something
> **a ward:** an area in a hospital where people who need medical treatment stay
> **a device:** a machine or an object that does a special job

1. My mother is in a small hospital _____ with just a few other patients.
2. Unfortunately, the _____ has spread to his brain. He may not have long to live.
3. The doors have a _____ that detects movement, so they open automatically.
4. Every medical _____ needs to be tested many times before doctors can use it.
5. If their blood sugar level gets too low, people with diabetes could have a(n) _____ .
6. The doctor was able to _____ the type of the disease right away, so she was able to treat it.
7. Doctors use this special device to _____ small amounts of bacteria in hospitals.

**A** Read the Park Rules sign. Rewrite the rules using *be (not) supposed to*.

1. You are not supposed to litter.
2. _____
3. _____
4. _____
5. _____
6. _____
7. _____

**Park Rules**

1 Do not litter.
2 Do not leave fires unattended.
3 Do not make excessive noise.
4 Do not feed the wildlife.
5 Keep pets on a leash.
6 Stay on the trails.
7 Store food in animal-proof containers.

**B** Complete the email with the correct form of *be (not) supposed to* and the verb in parentheses.

From: Margaret    To: Lisa

Hi Lisa,

I know we __are supposed to meet__ you for dinner tomorrow, but can we reschedule? Last
     **1 (meet)**
week, Matt and I went hiking for the first time at our local park, and you'll never guess what

happened! We didn't know we _____ off the trails, and we got lost. After
             **2 (walk)**

a while, we saw a beautiful lake in front of us and decided to take a swim, but we didn't know

that we _____ in the lake. While we were swimming, a bear came out of the
    **3 (swim)**
woods and took our bags. When we finally found our bags, all of our food was gone. We didn't

know that we _____ our food in animal-proof containers. By then, it was
       **4 (store)**
starting to get late, and we couldn't find our way out of the park, so we decided to light a fire. We

didn't know that we _____ the fire unattended, and we left it for a while to
      **5 (leave)**
look for the trail. When we got back, the fire had started to spread, so we got scared. I knew that

I _____ excessive noise, but I started yelling for help. Suddenly, a dog ran
 **6 (make)**
toward us out of nowhere. Its owner _____ it on a leash, but he hadn't. The
           **7 (keep)**
owner helped us to put the fire out and find the trail. As we were walking out of the park, Matt fell

and sprained his ankle. The doctor told Matt to stay off his ankle for a few days. So, I don't think

we can meet for dinner until next week. I hope we can see you then!

Best wishes,

Margaret

**C** MAKE IT PERSONAL Think about a swimming pool or lake near you. Write three of the rules using *be (not) supposed to*.

1. You're not supposed to run near the pool.
2. _____
3. _____
4. _____

# UNIT 4, LESSON 2    FUTURE CONTINUOUS

**A** Complete the online chat with the correct form of the future continuous.

Home | Discussion Board | Logout

**@Steve**

Hey, Jim! What ___will you be doing___ for spring break next month? Jake and I
_____ a seven-day trip to the Bahamas. Do you want to join us? If you do,
**2 (take)**
this time next month, we _____ in the ocean and snorkeling next to some
**3 (swim)**
beautiful fish. And you know what we won't be doing, right? We _____!
**4 (not study)**
Come on! It'll be lots of fun.

**@Jim**

Hey, Steve. It sounds like you _____ lots of cool things in the Bahamas,
**5 (do)**
but I don't think I can join you. I _____ my spring break with my family.
**6 (spend)**
We _____ to the mountains. So, unfortunately, I _____
**7 (go)**                                                        **8 (not snorkel)**
or swimming in the ocean, but I _____ lots of fun. Enjoy your trip!
**9 (have)**

**B** Complete the email with the words in the box. Use the correct continuous form.

| wait | fly | ~~pack~~ | talk | stay | take | walk |

From: Sarah    To: Su-jin

Hey Su-jin,

Sorry I haven't emailed you back yet! I ___was packing___ my bags all day yesterday and didn't have
**1**
time to write. Now I _____ for my plane at the airport, so I finally have a chance to email
**2**
you. I'm so excited to be visiting you in South Korea! I can't believe that this time tomorrow, we
_____ along the streets of Seoul. I'm sure that we _____ and laughing about
**3**                                                    **4**
all the good times we had at university. After I stay with you, I _____ the train from Seoul
**5**
to Busan. I _____ with another university friend for a week. Then I _____ back
**6**                                                                        **7**
home. I'd better go now because everyone is getting on the plane.
See you soon!
Best,
Sarah

**C** MAKE IT PERSONAL Write about something interesting you will be doing tomorrow,
next week, and next year.

1. Tomorrow, _I'll be hanging out with some old friends from high school._
2. Tomorrow, _____
3. Next week, _____
4. Next year, _____

# UNIT 4, LESSON 3   REDUCED RESTRICTIVE RELATIVE CLAUSES

**A** Combine the sentences using a reduced restrictive relative clause.

1. The trails had a lot of litter. We cleaned up the trails.
   <u>The trails we cleaned up had a lot of litter.</u>

2. The snorkeling tour included a visit to a coral reef. We took the tour last year.
   _____

3. The glacier is melting rapidly. Scientists are concerned about the glacier.
   _____

4. The river is contaminated. We have a sample of the river.
   _____

5. Don't drink the water. We haven't filtered the water.
   _____

6. A research paper on climate change won an award. I wrote the paper.
   _____

**B** MAKE IT PERSONAL Write sentences about what you can do at home to help the environment. Use reduced restrictive relative clauses.

1. <u>I can turn off all the lights and electronics I'm not using.</u>
2. _____
3. _____
4. _____

# UNIT 4, LESSON 4  VOCABULARY PRACTICE

Read the definitions. Then complete the sentences with the words.

> **exotic:** unusual or exciting because it is different or foreign
> **luxury:** very expensive, beautiful, and high quality
> **gourmet:** food or drink that is very high quality
> **world-class:** among the best in the world
> **cuisine:** food that is cooked in a particular style or place
> **stroll:** to walk in a slow, relaxed way
> **rugged:** rough, uneven, and with a lot of rocks

1. The new restaurant downtown has a(n) _____ chef. He's won many international awards.
2. Southern Italy is famous for its delicious _____ .
3. Some people like familiar foods better than _____ ones. They don't really like trying anything new.
4. This _____ hotel has a sauna and a golf course, but it costs more than $500 per night.
5. Expensive hotel restaurants often have great views and handmade, _____ food.
6. The _____ cliffs next to the river are very dangerous to climb.
7. In the evening, it is relaxing to _____ along the beach.

**136** GRAMMAR PRACTICE / VOCABULARY PRACTICE

**A** Complete the sentences with the past perfect continuous form of the verbs in parentheses.

1. I ____had been writing____ my essay when the battery in my laptop died.
(write)

2. We _____ for very long when the hard drive crashed.
(not / work)

3. _____ you _____ these problems before you
(have)
started your presentation?

4. Before the battery died, the computer _____ the professor
(not / give)
any problems.

5. She _____ to log in when the screen froze.
(try)

6. The student _____ strange error messages for a while before the tech
(get)
guy scanned the computer.

**B** Read Maria's email about her problems with technology. Circle the correct form of the verbs.

From: **Maria**    To: **Robbie**

Dear Robbie,

What a day! I **(1) had already been having** / had already had a few problems with my phone,
and I remembered that you **(2) had been having / having** a few problems with your phone when
it broke completely. So today after I'd **(3) been charging / charged** it completely and the screen
froze, I wasn't surprised. I breathed deeply and walked away from it for ten minutes.

When I **(4) returned / had been returning**, it seemed fine, so I left the house. By the time I got to
work, the screen **(5) had been freezing / had frozen** again! I nearly screamed!

I **(6) had already made / already made** an appointment at the phone repair center, so I took the
phone in during my lunch break. The tech guy told me he'd restored the phone settings, and I shouldn't
have any more problems. I paid and left the shop feeling happy to have a working phone again.

You'll never guess what happened next. I had met a co-worker as I was
returning to the office, and I **(7) telling / had been telling** her that the
problem was solved when my phone rang. I was just getting it out of my
bag when a man rushed by and knocked the phone out of my hand.
It landed hard on the sidewalk. When I picked it up, the screen was
broken. I nearly cried! I guess I'll be buying a new phone!

Best,

Maria

**C** MAKE IT PERSONAL Write sentences about technology problems you have had at home,
school, or work. Use the past perfect continuous.

1. _I had been watching a movie when the screen froze._

2. _____

3. _____

4. _____

**A** Rewrite each sentence using *need* + gerund or *need* + passive infinitive.

1. First, your cable needs to be replaced.
   First, your cable needs replacing.

2. His password needs resetting.
   _____

3. Does your device need restarting?
   _____

4. Her battery doesn't need to be recharged.
   _____

5. Their settings need to be restored.
   _____

6. Did that program need to be uninstalled?
   _____

7. Some new software needs to be installed.
   _____

**B** Complete the conversations with the correct form of the verbs in the box. More than one answer may be possible.

| install   replace   ~~restart~~   reconnect   reset   reboot   delete |
|---|

1. A: My screen froze.
   B: I think your computer needs to be _____ restarted _____.
2. A: Do you know where I can get another power cord?
   B: Are you sure your power cord needs _____? It looks brand new.
3. A: Does antivirus software need to be _____ on this computer?
   B: Definitely. It's the only way to protect your computer from viruses.
4. A: I was looking at this website and the internet stopped working.
   B: It's no problem. You just need to be _____ to the network.
5. A: I lost my password and I can't log in to my computer.
   B: Your password just needs _____.
6. A: Did the hard drive need _____?
   B: Yes. I shut the computer down and started it again, so everything is working now.
7. A: I don't have any more space on my hard drive.
   B: I think some of your files need to be _____.

**C** MAKE IT PERSONAL What local neighborhood problems need solutions? Write sentences using *need(s)* + gerund or *need(s)* + passive infinitive.

1. The windows in some of the buildings need to be replaced.
2. _____
3. _____
4. _____

# UNIT 5, LESSON 3    INFINITIVES AS SUBJECT COMPLEMENTS

**A** Complete the sentences with the correct form of the verbs in parentheses.

1. Our plan _____is to make_____ some workplace changes.
   (be / make)
2. Our goal has _____ happier employees.
   (be / have)
3. The first step will _____ a more flexible workspace.
   (be / create)
4. Our vision _____ the technology each employee uses.
   (be / improve)
5. One of the new ideas _____ employees to work from home every Friday.
   (be / allow)
6. The effect will _____ productivity and job satisfaction.
   (be / increase)

**B** MAKE IT PERSONAL Think about technology. Then complete the sentences with your ideas. Use an infinitive phrase.

1. My advice _is to take regular breaks from screens._
2. My advice _____
3. The important thing _____
4. The purpose of technology _____

# UNIT 5, LESSON 4  VOCABULARY PRACTICE

Read the definitions. Then complete the sentences with the words.

> **justified:** having an acceptable explanation or reason
> **expose:** to reveal the truth about something that is not acceptable
> **corruption:** dishonest or illegal behavior, especially from someone with power
> **confidential:** spoken or written in secret, and meant to be kept secret
> **outweigh:** to be more important or valuable than something else
> **privacy:** the state of being able to keep your life secret
> **jeopardize:** to risk losing or destroying something important

1. You don't want to _____ your friendship with him by publishing that story online, do you?
2. Both sides agreed to keep their financial agreement _____ .
3. Do the benefits of putting security cameras everywhere _____ the possible harms?
4. The actor said that the magazine invaded his _____ by publishing photos of him on vacation.
5. The judge decided that only a few of his complaints about being treated unfairly were _____ .
6. Reporters worked for years to _____ the truth about the government's secret program.
7. When millions of dollars disappeared, the leader of the organization was accused of _____ .

**A** Look at the picture. Write the answer to each question in the passive.

1. Who made the mug?
   <u>The mug was made by Sarah Field.</u>

2. When was the mug made?
   _____

3. What is the mug made of?
   _____

4. Where was the mug made?
   _____

5. When was the mug sold?
   _____

6. How is the mug used?
   _____

**Made by:**
Sarah Field
**Material:** glass
**Year made:** 1995
**Location made:**
Canada

**Year sold:**
2005
**Current use:**
to hold flowers

**B** Complete the conversation with the simple past passive. Use the verbs in parentheses.

Jenn:  Hey Jim, do you remember that famous antique shop we ___<u>were told</u>___ about?
       **1 (tell)**

Jim:   Yeah, it's called Asian Antiques, right?

Jenn:  Yep, that's it over there, isn't it? Let's check it out.

Jim:   Wow, there are so many cool things in here. Look at these giant bowls. Where do you think they _____?
       **2 (make)**

Jenn:  Maybe in China? They have such cool designs. I wonder if they

       _____ by hand.
       **3 (paint)**

Jim:   They probably were. They probably _____ to hold rice back then.
       **4 (use)**

Jenn:  Right. How old do you think they are?

Jim:   I'm not sure. Let's ask the owner.

Jenn:  Excuse me. How old are these bowls?

Store owner:  They're more than 100 years old. A friend of mine said that they

       _____ by a Chinese artist around 1900.
       **5 (design)**

Jenn:  Cool!

Store owner:  They're very popular. One _____ about an hour ago.
              **6 (buy)**

Jim:   Let's get a couple of them then. We can give them to our friends.

**C** MAKE IT PERSONAL  Think of a famous work of art. Write sentences to describe it using the simple present passive or simple past passive.

1. <u>The Mona Lisa was painted by Leonardo da Vinci.</u>
2. _____
3. _____
4. _____

**A** Complete the conversation with relative pronouns. More than one answer may be possible.

Ryan: Hey, Donna. Did you see last night's episode of *Singing Stars*? It's the only show
_____that_____ I'm really excited about this year.
 1

Donna: Yeah, I loved it, especially the woman _____ was wearing the red hat.
 2
Did you like her?

Ryan: Yeah. She had such a powerful voice. She also looked just like my friend Rachel,
_____ I met at college.
 3

Donna: Interesting.

Ryan: And she grew up in the same small town _____ my grandparents used to live.
 4

Donna: Cool!

Ryan: Yeah. What did you think of the guy _____ sang that country song?
 5

Donna: Oh, I don't think I saw him. He must have come on after 8:30, _____
 6
was when my mom called me.

Ryan: Oh.

Donna: Yeah, she usually calls me at 7:30, _____ is great because it's just after I eat
 7
dinner. But last night, she was busy, so she had to call me later.

Ryan: Well, I don't think you missed anything. He wasn't very good.

Donna: I can't wait for the next episode, _____ is supposed to be the finale.
 8

Ryan: Who do you think will win?

Donna: I'm not sure, but the girl from California, _____ is my favorite, has a
 9
good chance.

Ryan: Right! I like her, too.

**B** Reread the conversation in Exercise A. Look at the relative clauses. Write *R* if the clause is restrictive or *NR* if the clause is non-restrictive.

1. __R__       4. _____       7. _____
2. _____      5. _____       8. _____
3. _____      6. _____       9. _____

**C** MAKE IT PERSONAL Write about three friends and the music they like or don't like. Use restrictive and non-restrictive relative clauses.

1. My friend Tim, who I met in high school, loves jazz.
2. _____
3. _____
4. _____

**A** Complete the conversations with *can*, *can't*, *could*, or *couldn't* and the words in parentheses.

1. **A:** Is smoking permitted in this restaurant?
   **B:** No, absolutely not. <u>You can't smoke</u> (you / smoke) in any restaurants in this city.
2. **A:** Is it possible to order this dish without meat?
   **B:** Yes, of course. _____ (they / make) a vegetarian version.
3. **A:** Is fresh fruit available in the winter?
   **B:** Yes, _____ (you / get) all kinds of fresh fruit then.
4. **A:** Is there a Thai or Vietnamese restaurant around here?
   **B:** No, but _____ (you / find) many other international restaurants nearby.
5. **A:** Did the farmer's market have a lot of good vegetables?
   **B:** Not really. Unfortunately, _____ (they / grow) many crops last month because of the drought.
6. **A:** This town has a lot of really good Indian restaurants. Has it always been this way?
   **B:** No, not at all. Just a few years ago, _____ (you / have) Indian food unless you drove all the way to the city.

**B** MAKE IT PERSONAL Write sentences about restaurants where you live. Use *you* or *they* with *can / can't*, *could / couldn't* to express general truths.

1. <u>You can find cuisine from all over the world in my city.</u>
2. _____
3. _____
4. _____

# UNIT 6, LESSON 4  VOCABULARY PRACTICE

Read the definitions. Then complete the sentences with the words.

> **a dress code:** a set of rules about what you should wear in a place or situation
> **prohibit:** to not allow something
> **a loophole:** a small opening in a rule or law that people can use to avoid doing what the rule or law says
> **a controversy:** a serious disagreement about an issue
> **a garment:** a piece of clothing
> **a trend:** a way of thinking or doing something that is becoming more popular
> **the norm:** the usual way of doing something

1. The government passed a new law to _____ people from smoking in public places.
2. Some people follow every new fashion _____ set by celebrities.
3. The company took advantage of a _____ in the law to avoid paying more taxes.
4. Working from home is becoming the _____ for many employees in the US.
5. The school's decision to make students wear uniforms created a big _____ .
6. According to the company's new _____ , men have to wear collared shirts and ties at all times.
7. The tailor will repair the hole in your _____ and return it in three to five days.

# UNIT 7, LESSON 1 COMPARISONS WITH GERUND AND NOUN PHRASES

**A** Complete each conversation with the correct comparative form of the adjective in parentheses. More than one answer may be possible.

1. A: Did you like the flight crew on the plane?

   B: Yes, they were __friendlier than__ the crew on my last flight.
   **(friendly)**

2. A: Do you prefer takeoff or landing?

   B: To me, takeoff is _____ landing.
   **(scary)**

3. A: Are you going to fly business class?

   B: No, I'm flying economy. It is _____ business class.
   **(expensive)**

4. A: How is your seat?

   B: I think this seat is much _____ that one.
   **(comfortable)**

5. A: Are you going to get your boarding pass at the airport?

   B: No. Printing it at home is much _____ getting it at the airport.
   **(easy)**

6. A: Is taking a taxi to the airport _____ taking the bus?
   **(fast)**

   B: Yes, a taxi takes only thirty minutes.

**B** Complete the conversation with the correct form of the adjectives from the box.

> relaxing   expensive   fun   useful   close   ~~cheap~~

Travel agent: How would you prefer to travel?

Jim:    Umm…I'd prefer to travel by train. I've heard that it is ___cheaper___ than flying or
        taking the bus.
        **1**

Karen:  What? I think the train would be _____ than the bus.
        **2**

TA:  Let's worry about the transportation later. Let's concentrate on what you'd like to do
     because brainstorming is much _____ than arguing.
     **3**

K:  You're right. I'd like to do _____ activities, like getting a traditional massage.
    **4**

J:  But isn't traveling around _____ and exciting than lying around doing nothing?
    **5**

K:  Well, how about we choose a place where we can do a little bit of both?

TA:  How about Indonesia? There are plenty of opportunities for adventure and the beaches
     are beautiful. It's also much _____ than a lot of other countries, so you can get
     **6**
     there faster.

J and K: Great!

**C** MAKE IT PERSONAL Write sentences comparing traveling with friends and traveling alone.

1. _Traveling with friends is more fun than traveling alone._
2. _____
3. _____
4. _____

GRAMMAR PRACTICE   143

**A** Complete the sentences. Use *used to* or *would*. More than one answer may be possible.

1. My family __used to / would__ take a road trip every summer.
2. We _____ visit my grandmother's house in the mountains.
3. She _____ live next to a big lake.
4. In the evening, my grandmother _____ cook amazing food.
5. At night, everyone _____ sit around the fire.
6. My grandfather _____ tell funny stories.
7. I _____ think he was the best storyteller in the world.
8. Afterwards, we _____ go inside and watch movies.
9. The next morning, we _____ wake up and do it all over again.

**B** Rewrite the sentences. Replace *used to* with *would* when possible. If *would* cannot be used, write an *X* on the line.

1. My grandparents used to live in Orlando, Florida.
   _____X_____
2. Every summer, my family used to take the train to Florida.
   _____
3. We used to get on board early in the morning.
   _____
4. We used to eat breakfast, lunch, and dinner on the train.
   _____
5. I used to think that it was the best food in the world.
   _____
6. At night, we were so excited that we used to stay up all night.
   _____
7. We used to play card games and read books.
   _____
8. We used to love looking out the window.
   _____
9. I used to feel so happy on these trips.
   _____

**C** MAKE IT PERSONAL Write sentences about what you *would do / used to do* every summer when you were growing up.

1. Every summer, _I used to go swimming with my friends._____
2. Every summer, _____
3. Every summer, _____
4. Every summer, _____

# UNIT 7, LESSON 3   *IT* + PAST PASSIVE

**A** Rewrite each sentence using *it* + past passive. Remember the subject is not needed in the passive sentence.

1. People once believed that airships would be a popular method of transportation.
   It was once believed that airships would be a popular method of transportation.
2. Many experts thought that every city would have streetcars.

3. People expected that supersonic flights would become common.

4. Science fiction writers predicted that we would all have flying cars.

5. Many experts once said that train travel would not work.

6. Some people believed that airplanes would just be a fad.


**B** MAKE IT PERSONAL  What predictions from the past do you remember? Write sentences using *it* + past passive.

1. It was expected that there would be no more poverty by the year 2000.
2. 
3. 
4. 

# UNIT 7, LESSON 4  VOCABULARY PRACTICE

Read the definitions. Then complete the sentences with the words.

**transport**: to move people or things from one place to another
**mountainous**: having a lot of very high hills, mountains
**horizontal**: flat and level
**escalator**: moving stairs that carry people up and down
**practical**: useful for a specific purpose
**a commute**: a regular trip to and from a place, particularly work
**steep**: at a sharp angle making it difficult to climb

1. Sometimes walking somewhere is more _____ than driving, especially when there isn't a place to park your car.
2. The northern part of the country is really _____ , so it's great for hiking and skiing.
3. My _____ to work takes me about forty-five minutes each way.
4. When I'm tired, I prefer to take the _____ instead of climbing the stairs.
5. That part of the mountain is too _____ for most hikers to climb.
6. The company uses huge trucks to _____ its equipment from place to place.
7. The railroad tracks stretched out for kilometers in a _____ direction.

GRAMMAR PRACTICE / VOCABULARY PRACTICE   145

# UNIT 8, LESSON 1    MODALS FOR PAST REGRETS AND POSSIBILITIES

**A** Complete the sentences with the correct form of the modals in parentheses.

1. She ___should have kept___ her cool.
   (should keep)
2. I _____ my voice. I'm sorry.
   (should / not / raise)
3. She _____ it to work on time if she had left her house earlier.
   (could / make)
4. They _____ nicer to me. They were so easy to deal with.
   (could / not / be)
5. Jenny _____. I think she was just having a bad day.
   (might / overreact)
6. There was no need to yell. We _____ it over calmly.
   (should / talk)
7. It's not a big deal that the children didn't go to bed earlier. You _____
   (should / not / be)
   so hard on them.
8. It's a good thing we didn't wait until today to send the package or it
   _____ in time for her birthday.
   (might / not / arrived)

**B** Circle the correct form of the modal.

Ruth: Hey, Stacy! You'll never believe what happened today.
Stacy: Hey, Ruth. I'm really sorry I (1) _couldn't make_ / could make it to the meeting. What happened?
Ruth: Well, Richard and Carl got into a huge argument.
Stacy: Whoa! That's not like them. They must have been really angry!
Ruth: Yep, but they (2) should have / shouldn't have started yelling at each other in front of everyone.
Stacy: True. They (3) shouldn't keep / should have kept their cool.
Ruth: And Tim just stood there watching them. He didn't do anything! He really (4) should deal with / should have dealt with it right away.
Stacy: Definitely. But he (5) might be / might have been a little scared. I know I (6) would be / would have been!
Ruth: Yeah, we all were.
Stacy: Well, they must be really embarrassed now.
Ruth: They (7) should be / should have been! I hope everything is OK between them before the next meeting!

**C** MAKE IT PERSONAL Read the scenario. Write sentences about what you could have or should have done to handle the situation better. Use past modals.

Your friend arrived very late at the airport to pick you up. Your friend didn't call or say anything about being late, so when he / she arrived you lost your temper without asking for an explanation. Then you took a taxi home. Now, your friend isn't talking to you.

1. I shouldn't have overreacted.
2. _____
3. _____
4. _____

**A** Rewrite the sentences using *wish* and *if only*.

1. I'm not fluent in Spanish. (if only)
   <u>If only I were fluent in Spanish.</u>

2. I didn't complete my work on time. (wish)
   _____

3. I don't spend time learning math. (wish)
   _____

4. We didn't commit to our exercise plan. (if only)
   _____

5. They're not skilled at cooking. (wish)
   _____

6. You didn't get a handle on the new program. (if only)
   _____

**B** Complete the conversations with the correct form of the verbs in parentheses.

1. A: Have you started taking Spanish classes?

   B: No, not yet. I really wish I ____<u>had started</u>____ taking them last year.
   **(start)**

2. A: Do you go to the gym every day?

   B: No. If only I _____ every day, I'd feel a lot fitter by now.
   **(go)**

3. A: Are you coming to the game this Saturday?

   B: No, I'm sorry. I wish I _____ able to go, but I promised to study with
   **(be)**
   my friend.

4. A: I wish I _____ more skilled at using the computer.
   **(be)**

   B: Me, too! Then this project wouldn't take so long.

5. A: Hey! Let's swim to the island!

   B: I'm not that good at swimming. If only I _____ to swim when I
   **(learn)**
   was younger.

6. A: Did you make the cake yourself?

   B: No, I bought it from a bakery. I wish I _____ cakes like this!
   **(could / bake)**

7. A: Did you hear that the Smiths went to Hawaii last week?

   B: Yeah. I wish we _____ with them!
   **(could / go)**

**C** MAKE IT PERSONAL What are your wishes for right now, last year, and next year?
Write sentences using *wish* and *if only*.

1. (right now) <u>I wish I were a better singer.</u>
2. (right now) _____
3. (last year) _____
4. (next year) _____

**A** Read David's wish list. The complete the sentences using *more than* or *less than*.

David's wish list for next year, in order of importance:
| | |
|---|---|
| 1. Visit relatives in Tokyo | 5. Buy a new car |
| 2. Enroll in graduate school | 6. Run a marathon |
| 3. Get a promotion at work | 7. Go on a beach excursion with friends |
| 4. Travel to Europe | 8. Take a cooking class |

1. David cares about enrolling in graduate school ____more than he cares about____ buying a new car.
2. He wants to get a promotion at work _____ travel to Europe.
3. He cares about buying a new car _____ visiting his relatives.
4. He'd like to visit his relatives in Tokyo _____ go on a beach excursion with his friends.
5. He is concerned about running a marathon _____ enrolling in graduate school.
6. He wants to run a marathon _____ take a cooking class.

**B** MAKE IT PERSONAL Write sentences comparing items on your wish list for the next year. Use *more than* or *less than*.

1. I care about finding a fulfilling job more than I care about the salary.
2. _____
3. _____
4. _____

# UNIT 8, LESSON 4  VOCABULARY PRACTICE

Read the definitions. Then complete the sentences with the words.

**rejection:** the act of saying or showing that you don't want something or someone
**assume:** to think something is true, even though you have no proof
**overcome:** to successfully deal with a feeling or problem that is stopping you from doing something
**an entrepreneur:** someone who starts and manages a company and takes risks to make a profit
**pursue:** to continue trying hard to do or achieve something
**therapy:** treatment to help you recover from mental or physical problems
**profound:** having a strong effect

1. The talk had a(n) _____ effect on me and changed how I think about the world.
2. He decided not to apply for the job because he was afraid of _____ .
3. People often _____ that the company is named after me, but it's actually named after my sister.
4. He went for _____ after one of his pets died, and now he feels much better.
5. He really wanted to _____ his fear of flying so he could travel more.
6. She quit her job after ten years to _____ her dream of opening her own restaurant.
7. After getting his degree, he started his own company and became a successful _____ .

**A** Complete the conversations with the correct form of the verbs in parentheses.

1. A: Would she mind _____brainstorming_____ with me?
      **(brainstorm)**
   B: I don't think so. Why don't you ask her?

2. A: Do you mind _____ this essay for me?
      **(edit)**
   B: I'm sorry, but I can't right now. I have too much to do at the moment.

3. A: Would you mind _____ my paper?
      **(look over)**
   B: Sure, but can I do it after I finish this?

4. A: Do you mind _____ on this before I keep going?
      **(give feedback)**
   B: OK. No problem.

5. A: Do you mind if I _____ this section a little?
      **(revise)**
   B: Hmm…I don't think that's necessary. It looks OK as it is.

6. A: Do you mind if I _____ this paper after lunch?
      **(submit)**
   B: Nope. That's fine. Take your time.

7. A: Do they mind _____ the proposal for us?
      **(draft)**
   B: I'm not sure. I can ask them later if you want.

**B** Read the sentences. Write polite questions to make requests or ask for permission.

1. My paper needs to be edited.
   Would _you mind editing my paper_____?

2. I need my paper to be looked over.
   Do _____?

3. I need help organizing my ideas.
   Do _____?

4. I want to submit this next week.
   Would _____?

5. I need help revising my paper.
   Would _____?

6. I want to brainstorm some new ideas.
   Do _____?

7. I need someone to double-check the facts in my essay.
   Would _____?

**C** MAKE IT PERSONAL  Write sentences asking your co-worker or friend for help or permission.

1. _Would you mind helping me with this report?_____

2. _____

3. _____

4. _____

# UNIT 9, LESSON 2    MODALS WITH THE PASSIVE

**A** Rewrite each sentence in the passive.

1. The company might make some big changes.
   <u>Some big changes might be made (by the company).</u>

2. The manager should hire some new employees.
   _____

3. The boss might fire Mike.
   _____

4. The CEO could promote Rachel.
   _____

5. The business might not lay off fifty workers.
   _____

6. The organization should not transfer Brian to a new department.
   _____

7. Should the group assign Jenny to a new project?
   _____

**B** Read the conversation. Complete the sentences with the correct form of the verbs in parentheses.

Dawn:   Did you hear that Robert <u>  might be fired  </u>?
                                          **1 (might / fire)**

Salma:   No. Really? What happened?

Dawn:   I heard that he _____ at a customer yesterday. I guess he was angry.
                                          **2 (might / yell)**

Salma:   That's too bad.

Dawn:   But guess who _____ to take his position?
                                          **3 (might / promote)**

Salma:   Who?

Dawn:   Ted!

Salma:   Really? I thought the manager _____ Brad to take that position.
                                          **4 (might / chose)**

Dawn:   Honestly, Ali _____ the one to get it.
                                          **5 (should / be)**

Salma:   You're right. Ali is such a hard worker. But I heard that he _____
                                                                  **6 (could / transfer)**
       to a different department soon.

Dawn:   I also heard that the manager is thinking about giving Robert another chance.

Salma:   I _____ pretty happy if I were Robert.
               **7 (might / be)**

**C** MAKE IT PERSONAL Write about things that could, should, or might happen to you in the next month. Use modals with passive infinitives.

1. <u>I might be promoted next month.</u>
2. _____
3. _____
4. _____

**A** Rewrite the sentences using the words in parentheses + an infinitive.

1. Jim won't get a promotion unless he works harder. (not likely)
   <u>Jim is not likely to get a promotion unless he works harder.</u>

2. You will pass the exam if you study. (certain)
   _____

3. We will find a solution to the problem if we work together. (likely)
   _____

4. A candidate who speaks Chinese will get the position. (more likely)
   _____

5. If you don't get enough sleep, you won't do well on your interview. (less likely)
   _____

6. Our company will reorganize its staff this year. (almost certain)
   _____

**B** MAKE IT PERSONAL  Write sentences about what you are likely to do and what you are certain to do in the next five years. Use *likely* or *certain* + an infinitive.

1. <u>I am likely to get a promotion at my company.</u>
2. _____
3. _____
4. _____

# UNIT 9, LESSON 4  VOCABULARY PRACTICE

Read the definitions. Then complete the sentences with the words.

> **realistic:** based on what is real or possible
> **satisfying:** making you feel pleased or happy
> **a requirement:** something that someone needs or asks for
> **a salary:** money you receive regularly for the work you do
> **a quality:** a good or bad part of someone's character
> **open-minded:** willing to consider and accept other people's ideas and opinions

1. I get to use my skills to make people happy, so I find my work very _____ .
2. Having a university degree is just one _____ for this job.
3. Most of his _____ is spent on food, rent, and transportation.
4. His best _____ is the fact that he is always honest.
5. My boss is very _____ . He always listens to me and tries to accept my suggestions.
6. It's fun to have big dreams, but it is also important to set _____ goals.

**A** Read the sentences. Add *do, does,* or *did* for emphasis. Change the main verb if necessary.

1. Please, have another cup of tea.
   Please, do have another cup of tea.

2. They restored the old building.
   _____

3. He went to the amphitheater.
   _____

4. They redeveloped the waterfront.
   _____

5. Visit the large fountain.
   _____

6. The waterfront looks much better now.
   _____

7. They tore down the old hotel.
   _____

8. She constructs beautiful buildings.
   _____

9. It looks like an important landmark.
   _____

**B** Complete the sentences with the correct form of *do, does,* or *did*. Then check (✓) the sentences in which *do, does,* or *did* is used for emphasis.

1. They _____did_____ restore that amphitheater. ✓
2. _____ the same company just renovate both buildings? ☐
3. They _____ construct that building last year. ☐
4. She _____ love that plaza, doesn't she? ☐
5. That fountain _____ stop working in 1977. ☐
6. Wow! My teacher _____ not tell me about that landmark! ☐
7. They _____ not restore the old painting yet. ☐
8. She _____ go to the waterfront. I saw her there! ☐
9. _____ he want to come with us? Let's ask him now. ☐

**C** MAKE IT PERSONAL Think about the last time you visited a different city. Write about things you did or didn't do there. Use *do* or *did* for emphasis.

1. I didn't watch a basketball game, but I did go to the aquarium.
2. _____
3. _____
4. _____

# UNIT 10, LESSON 2   PAST PERFECT WITH ADVERBIAL CLAUSES OF TIME

**A** Complete the conversation with the correct form of the verbs in parentheses.

A: When we _____arrived_____ at the train station, the train
        **1 (arrive)**
_____ already.
      **2 (leave)**

B: Oh, no!

A: Wait. It gets better. By the time we _____ someone to help us,
                                              **3 (find)**
we _____ the next train, too! So, we were stuck at the train station
       **4 (miss)**
waiting for six hours for the next available train.

B: That sounds awful!

A: Yep, it was! By the time we _____ home, we _____
                                  **5 (arrive)**                          **6 (traveled)**
a total of twenty hours.

B: Oh! You must have been exhausted! That happened to me once. By the time we

_____ at the airport, our airplane _____. We had to wait
      **7 (arrive)**                                    **8 (take off)**
until the next day to catch another flight.

A: That's not fun. I'm sorry you had that experience.

**B** Rewrite the sentences using the words in parentheses.

1. When we pulled into the garage, she had already left. (by the time)
   _By the time we pulled into the garage, she had already left._

2. As soon as I had crossed the bridge, the light turned red. (after)
   _____

3. By the time I got off the train, the rain had already stopped. (before)
   _____

4. When she called, we had already pulled out of the driveway. (by the time)
   _____

5. By the time he got to the theater, the movie had already ended. (when)
   _____

6. As soon as he had finished his breakfast, he headed out to the store. (once)
   _____

7. Before he pulled in, they had already started eating. (by the time)
   _____

8. Before I got to the office, the meeting had already started. (when)
   _____

**C** MAKE IT PERSONAL  Imagine that you missed your train. Write sentences about what happened next. Use the past perfect with adverbial clauses of time.

1. By the time _I got to the station, I had already missed my train._
2. By the time _____
3. As soon as _____
4. When _____

# UNIT 10, LESSON 3  NON-RESTRICTIVE RELATIVE CLAUSES FOR COMMENTS

**A** Combine the two sentences. Use the second sentence as a non-restrictive relative clause.

1. I went to an art exhibition with my sister. It was a lot of fun.
   I went to an art exhibition with my sister, which was a lot of fun.

2. I left my jacket on the bus. That was a big mistake.
   _____

3. My wallet was in the pocket. That was unfortunate.
   _____

4. My sister told me to call the lost and found office. I hadn't thought of that.
   _____

5. Someone had brought my jacket to the office. That was very kind.
   _____

6. My wallet was still in the pocket. That was really lucky.
   _____

**B** MAKE IT PERSONAL Write sentences about losing something. Use non-restrictive relative clauses to make a comment about each sentence.

1. I lost my keys today, which was really annoying.
2. _____
3. _____
4. _____

# UNIT 10, LESSON 4  VOCABULARY PRACTICE

Read the definitions. Then complete the sentences with the words.

> **lush:** growing well, healthy, and with a lot of green leaves
> **greenery:** plants and trees that are growing
> **eco-friendly:** good for the environment
> **a structure:** something that has been built
> **a commitment:** a promise to do something in a particular way
> **sustain:** to make something continue over a period of time
> **an impression:** the opinion or feeling you have about something because of what you see or hear
> **paradise:** a place that is very beautiful and enjoyable

1. After being in the cold city all winter, the tropical island felt like _____ .
2. They were planning to build a(n) _____ that was big enough to hold 100 people.
3. The company had a strong _____ to making conditions better for its employees.
4. In the rain forest, we were surrounded by trees and other kinds of _____ .
5. There has been no rain, so the _____ grass has started to turn brown.
6. The hotel room looked clean and bright, so our first _____ of it was good.
7. Companies are making _____ products that help to protect the environment.
8. We need to _____ our commitment so that it continues for a long time.

### Reaching the Peak

How can Yuzuru Hanyu do those amazing spins and jumps on the ice? How does Serena Williams win so many tennis tournaments? How is Lionel Messi able make so many goals? You might think the answer is "practice, practice, practice," but according to a new study from psychologist Brooke Macnamara, you would
5  be wrong. Practice is important for all athletes, of course, but there are other things that make the difference between being good and being one of the best. To reach peak performance, athletes need to watch their diets carefully, get plenty of sleep, and achieve the right state of mind. And when you think about it, those are habits we could all benefit from.

Top athletes know that their bodies need the right fuel. For them, diet is not about body shape—it's about
10  strength, endurance, and energy levels. Of course, their diets vary a lot. Williams eats a lot of nuts, beans, and fruit. Hanyu has soup with pork and soy before every competition. In addition to healthy food, a good diet also includes good hydration. It's important for athletes to get plenty of water and other fluids. The best athletes know that everything they put into their bodies affects their performance.

When athletes train for six hours a day, six days a week, it does a lot of damage to their muscles, and sleep
15  is the only way to repair that damage. Athletes need eight to ten hours of sleep a night—more sleep than the average person. Messi often gets twelve! And many top athletes make an extra effort to get deep, high-quality sleep. A very dark room and cool temperatures are the solution for some. Others use a fan or a white noise machine to block out other sounds. Their specific habits may vary, but all elite athletes know that they need a good night's sleep every night to be at their best.

20  Finally, the right mental state can make the difference between a good performance and peak performance. Many athletes prepare for competitions by concentrating on positive thoughts or repeating calming words to themselves. They also work hard to keep a positive attitude about the endless hours of training. They make an active effort to enjoy improving their skills rather than just viewing training as a means to an end. And when they are injured, they don't let it get them down but instead focus on what's necessary for recovery. When
25  Hanyu was injured, he continued preparing for the next Olympics with visualization exercises—imagining himself doing his jumps. Many athletes will say that these habits of mental discipline are what put them on top of their game.

For elite athletes, the commitment to peak performance affects every part of their lives. From what they eat for breakfast to when they go to bed at night to how they deal with stress, every habit can make a difference.
30  That's how they make leaping on the ice or slamming the ball over the net look so easy. Most of us are not athletes, but we can apply some of their strategies for success in our own lives.

# REFERENCES

## UNIT 2, LESSON 1      FUTURE REAL CONDITIONAL

Use the future real conditional to talk about what will likely happen under certain conditions. The *if*-clause gives the condition.

**Statements**

| *If*-clause | | | | Result clause | | | |
|------|---------|-------------------|----------------|---------|------------------|------------------|-----------|
| *If* | Subject | Simple present | | Subject | *Will / Won't* | Base form of verb | |
| | I | **feel** | sick, | I | **will** | **stay** | home. |
| **If** | you | **don't take** | this medicine, | you | **won't** | **get** | better. |
| | people | **get** | sick, | they | **will** | **miss** | work. |

**Questions**

| *If*-clause | | | | Result clause | | | | |
|------|---------|----------------|---------|----------|----------------|---------|-------------------|----------|
| *If* | Subject | Simple present | | *Wh*-word | *Will / Won't* | Subject | Base form of verb | |
| **If** | you | **feel** | sick, | who | **will** | you | **call**? | |
| | he | **gets** | better, | – | **will** | he | **come** | to work? |

**Note:** The *if*-clause can come at the beginning or end of a sentence. Use a comma when the *if*-clause comes at the beginning of a sentence.

*If you come to work,* you'll make others sick.     *You'll make other sick **if** you come to work.*

*If you feel sick,* will you come to work?      *Will you come to work **if** you feel sick?*

## UNIT 2, LESSON 1      *UNLESS*

Use *unless* to express condition. *Unless* often means *if…not.*

| *Unless* | Subject | Present verb | | Subject | Future verb or modal + verb | |
|----------|-------------|------------|------------|---------|----------------------------|----------------|
| | you | leave | soon, | you | are going to be | late. |
| **Unless** | the clients | trust | you, | they | won't want | your services. |
| | you | make | an effort, | you | can't | succeed. |

**Notes**

- When the verb in the main clause is in the future, use the simple present in the clause with *if*.
- You can start the sentence with the main clause.

  *We will meet at 9:00 unless the office is closed.*

# UNIT 2, LESSON 2     PRESENT UNREAL CONDITIONAL

Use present unreal conditionals to talk about untrue or imagined situations and their results.

**Statements**

| *If*-clause | | | | Result clause | | | |
|---|---|---|---|---|---|---|---|
| *If* | Subject | Simple past | | Subject | *Would / Wouldn't* | Base form of verb | |
| If | I | **were** | rich, | I | **would** | **donate** | more money. |
| | she | **had** | more time, | she | **would** | **volunteer** | every day. |
| | people | **didn't care,** | | they | **wouldn't** | **help**. | |

**Questions**

| *If*-clause | | | | Result clause | | | | |
|---|---|---|---|---|---|---|---|---|
| *If* | Subject | Simple past | | *Wh-word* | *Would / Wouldn't* | Subject | Base form of verb | |
| If | you | **had** | more money, | what | **would** | you | **do**? | |
| | they | **had** | the time, | – | **would** | they | **help** | us? |

**Note**

- The *if-clause* uses the simple past, but this is not a past statement. It's about the present.
- For the *be* verb, use *were* for all subjects: *If he* **were** *president… If they* **were** *free…*
- The *if-clause* can come at the beginning or end of a sentence. Use a comma when the *if-clause* comes at the beginning of a sentence.

# UNIT 3, LESSON 1     ADVICE, OBLIGATION, AND EXPECTATION

| | *(Not) have to / Had better (not) / Be (not) supposed to* | Base form of verb | | |
|---|---|---|---|---|
| Everyone | **has to** | come | to the meeting. | (It's required.) |
| You | **don't have to** | accept | that offer. | (You can walk away.) |
| I | **had better** | leave | now. | (I'm going to be late.) |
| You | **had better not** | be | late. | (The boss will be angry.) |
| I | **am supposed to** | call | them. | (They're expecting my call.) |
| We | **aren't supposed to** | use | our phones. | (It's against the rules.) |

**Notes**

- *Had better (not)* often carries a suggestion of bad consequences.
- Use *have to* to say that an action is necessary / required.
- Use *(not) have to* to say that an action is not necessary.
- Use *had better (not)* to give strong advice or to talk about things people should or shouldn't do.
- Use *be (not) supposed to* to express expectations.

## UNIT 4, LESSON 2    FUTURE WITH *WILL, BE GOING TO*, PRESENT CONTINUOUS, AND SIMPLE PRESENT

Use *will* + the base form of the verb for predictions, offers, and quick decisions made at the moment of speaking.

| Predictions | We're all excited about the project. I think tomorrow's meeting **will be** great. |
|---|---|
| Offers | Those boxes look heavy. We**'ll help** you carry them. |
| Quick decisions | That's a great price. I**'ll take** it! |

Use *be going to* + the base form of the verb for predictions and to talk about specific plans.

| Predictions | Bob just got a new apartment, and he**'s going to need** a lot of furniture. |
|---|---|
| Specific plans | We need a lot of furniture. We**'re going to go** shopping this weekend. |

Use the present continuous to talk about specific plans.

| Specific plans | I can't wait for the weekend. We**'re having** dinner with my cousins from Lima. |
|---|---|

Use the simple present for future events that are on a definite schedule, such as store hours, bus and train schedules, flight times, and movie showings.

| Definite schedules | His flight **gets** in at 9:00 on Sunday. |
|---|---|

## UNIT 5, LESSON 1    PAST PERFECT

Use the past perfect to talk about an action that occurred before another time in the past.

| | *Had* | Past participle | |
|---|---|---|---|
| The police discovered that the thief | **had** | **taken** | the painting. |
| Before the robbery, the gang | **had** | **dug** | a tunnel to the bank. |

**Notes**
- The past perfect is sometimes used with *before, after, by the time*, and *when*.
  ***By the time*** *police arrived, the robbers had already left.*
- We often use contractions with subject pronouns and *had* with the past perfect.
  *They**'d** robbed another bank earlier that week.*
- We also use the contraction *hadn't* with negative past perfect sentences.
  *They didn't stop the thief because they **hadn't** noticed the theft yet.*

# IRREGULAR VERBS

| Base form of verb | Simple past | Past participle | Base form of verb | Simple past | Past participle |
|---|---|---|---|---|---|
| be | was | been | leave | left | left |
| become | became | become | lay (off) | laid (off) | laid (off) |
| begin | began | begun | lose | lost | lost |
| break | broke | broken | make | made | made |
| bring | brought | brought | mean | meant | meant |
| build | built | built | meet | met | met |
| buy | bought | bought | oversleep | overslept | overslept |
| catch | caught | caught | pay | paid | paid |
| choose | chose | chosen | put | put | put |
| come | came | come | quit | quit | quit |
| cut | cut | cut | read | read | read |
| cost | cost | cost | ride | rode | ridden |
| deal | dealt | dealt | rise | rose | risen |
| do | did | done | run | run | run |
| draw | drew | drawn | say | said | said |
| drink | drank | drunk | see | saw | seen |
| drive | drove | driven | sell | sold | sold |
| eat | ate | eaten | send | sent | sent |
| fall | fell | fallen | set | set | set |
| feed | fed | fed | show | showed | shown |
| feel | felt | felt | shut | shut | shut |
| fight | fought | fought | sing | sang | sung |
| find | found | found | sit | sit | sit |
| fly | flew | flown | sleep | slept | slept |
| forget | forgot | forgotten | speak | spoke | spoken |
| forgive | forgave | forgiven | spend | spent | spent |
| freeze | froze | frozen | stand | stood | stood |
| get | got | gotten | steal | stole | stolen |
| give | gave | given | swim | swam | swum |
| go | went | gone | take | took | taken |
| grow | grew | grown | teach | taught | taught |
| have | had | had | tell | told | told |
| hear | heard | heard | think | thought | thought |
| hide | hid | hidden | understand | understood | understood |
| hit | hit | hit | wear | wore | worn |
| hold | held | held | win | won | won |
| know | knew | known | write | wrote | written |

# PREPOSITIONS

| | | | |
|---|---|---|---|
| about | below | from...to | outside |
| above | beneath | in | over |
| across | beside | in front of | past |
| after | besides | inside | round / around |
| against | between | in spite of | since |
| ahead of | beyond | into | than |
| along | but | like | through |
| among | by | near | throughout |
| apart from | concerning | next to | to |
| around | despite | of | towards |
| as | down | off | under |
| at | during | on | until |
| away from | except (for) | onto | up |
| because of | facing | on top of | with |
| before | for | opposite | within |
| behind | from | out of | without |

# PARTICIPIAL ADJECTIVES

| -ed | -ing | -ed | -ing | -ed | -ing |
|---|---|---|---|---|---|
| alarmed | alarming | disturbed | disturbing | moved | moving |
| amazed | amazing | embarrassed | embarrassing | paralyzed | paralyzing |
| amused | amusing | entertained | entertaining | pleased | pleasing |
| annoyed | annoying | excited | exciting | relaxed | relaxing |
| astonished | astonishing | exhausted | exhausting | satisfied | satisfying |
| bored | boring | fascinated | fascinating | shocked | shocking |
| charmed | charming | frightened | frightening | surprised | surprising |
| confused | confusing | horrified | horrifying | terrified | terrifying |
| depressed | depressing | inspired | inspiring | tired | tiring |
| disappointed | disappointing | interested | interesting | touched | touching |
| disgusted | disgusting | irritated | irritating | troubled | troubling |

# REPORTING VERBS

## Verbs for reporting what someone says

| | | | | | | |
|---|---|---|---|---|---|---|
| acknowledge | confess | dispute | invite | propose | request | tell |
| add | confirm | explain | maintain | reassure | respond | threaten |
| admit | continue | forbid | mention | recall | reveal | urge |
| advise | convince | guarantee | note | recommend | rule | warn |
| agree | cry | hint | notify | record | say | whisper |
| announce | demand | imply | observe | refuse | scream | write |
| answer | deny | inform | order | remark | shout | yell |
| argue | describe | inquire | persuade | remind | state | |
| ask | direct | insist | predict | repeat | suggest | |
| assert | discuss | instruct | promise | reply | teach | |

## Verbs for reporting what someone thinks

| | | | |
|---|---|---|---|
| accept | expect | know | remember |
| agree | fear | mean | resolve |
| assume | feel | note | suppose |
| believe | forget | plan | think |
| consider | guess | prefer | understand |
| decide | hold | propose | want |
| determine | hope | reason | wish |
| doubt | imagine | recall | wonder |
| dream | intend | reflect | worry |
| estimate | judge | regret | |

## Verbs for reporting what someone has written

| | | | |
|---|---|---|---|
| add | claim | insist | say |
| admit | command | observe | state |
| advise | comment | order | suggest |
| agree | complain | promise | tell |
| announce | conclude | read | think |
| answer | confess | reason | urge |
| argue | continue | reflect | warn |
| assert | decide | remark | wonder |
| beg | demand | reply | write |
| begin | explain | report | |
| boast | inquire | respond | |

# METRIC CONVERSIONS

| Volume | | Length and distance | | Weight | |
|---|---|---|---|---|---|
| 1 fluid ounce | 29.57 milliliters | 1 centimeter | .39 inch | 1 ounce | 28.35 grams |
| 1 milliliter | .034 fluid ounce | 1 inch | 2.54 centimeters | 1 gram | .04 ounce |
| 1 pint | .47 liter | 1 foot | .30 meter | 1 pound | .45 kilogram |
| 1 liter | 2.11 pints | 1 meter | 3.28 feet | 1 kilogram | 2.2 pounds |
| 1 quart | .95 liter | 1 yard | .91 meter | | |
| 1 liter | 1.06 quarts | 1 meter | 1.09 yards | | |
| 1 gallon | 3.79 liters | 1 mile | 1.61 kilometers | | |
| 1 liter | .26 gallon | 1 kilometer | .62 mile | | |

# THE WRITING PROCESS

The writing process consists of 5 stages:

1. Pre-writing
2. Drafting
3. Revising
4. Proofreading
5. Publishing

The five stages of the writing process can be applied to any type of writing task. Whether you are writing an essay, an article, or a blog entry, each stage allows your writing to progress from an idea in your head to a completed text. With each stage you shape and improve your writing.

| Pre-writing | PLAN |
|---|---|
| | ⇨ The Pre-writing stage is where you make a plan for your writing. |
| | ⇨ Choose a topic you want to write about. |
| | ⇨ Think about what you want to say about the topic. |
| | ⇨ Generate ideas using brainstorming techniques (mind maps, idea webs, lists, etc.). |
| | ⇨ Do research, if necessary, and take notes. |
| | ⇨ Use graphic organizers and charts to start arranging your ideas. |
| **Drafting** | WRITE |
| | ⇨ The Drafting stage is where you begin to turn your ideas into a written text. |
| | ⇨ Think about your audience. Your tone will vary if you are writing for students or business professionals or to a friend or a university professor. |
| | ⇨ Use ideas from the Pre-writing stage to start composing sentences and paragraphs. Don't focus too much on grammar and mechanics. Just get ideas flowing. |
| | ⇨ If using researched materials, put the information in your own words or use quotations. Keep track of the references you use. |
| | ⇨ First focus on the body of your text. Then add a beginning and ending. |
| | ⇨ Read your draft to see if what you're saying flows logically. |
| | ⇨ You may need to complete this stage more than once. |
| **Revising** | IMPROVE |
| | ⇨ The Revising stage helps you to improve tone, content, style, and organization. |
| | ⇨ Consider your target audience again and adjust the tone as needed. |
| | ⇨ Cut, add, change, and rearrange text as needed. |
| | ⇨ Develop an effective beginning and ending. |
| | ⇨ Check if you need to give more information about any details. |
| | ⇨ Vary words that you repeat too often. |
| | ⇨ Revisit the drafting steps to develop new ideas that need to be added. |
| | ⇨ Ask a friend or classmate to review your draft, and incorporate feedback that you find helpful. |
| | ⇨ Set your writing aside and then return to it with fresh eyes and read it again. |
| | ⇨ You may need to complete this stage more than once. |

| Proofreading | CORRECT |
|---|---|
| | ⇨ The Proofreading stage comes only after you are happy with tone, content, style, and organization. |
| | ⇨ Print your document before proofreading if you are working on a computer. You may notice mistakes that you can miss on a screen. |
| | ⇨ Look for errors in spelling, punctuation, and capitalization. Read your text several times, first focusing only on spelling, then on punctuation, then on capitalization. |
| | ⇨ Do several sweeps for grammar mistakes, checking for your individual problem areas. For example, first focus on sentence structure, then read again to check for subject-verb agreement, then again for use of tenses. |
| | ⇨ Check that you listed any references correctly. |
| | ⇨ Ask another person to proofread your text for you. Make sure you agree with the corrections and understand them before applying them. |
| | ⇨ Once you print a final copy, don't add hand-written corrections. Print a clean copy. |
| Publishing | SHARE |
| | ⇨ Finally, at the Publishing stage, you can share your text with other people. |
| | ⇨ Post it online. |
| | ⇨ Send it in an email or letter. |
| | ⇨ Present it orally to people. |
| | ⇨ Hand it in to a teacher or supervisor. |
| | ⇨ Submit it to a publication or a contest. |

# PRESENTATION SELF-EVALUATION

Fill out the evaluation after giving your presentation. If possible, ask a classmate to record your presentation. Then complete the chart after watching it. Be honest and keep notes of your observations to improve future presentations.

| Criteria | Goals | Self rating 1–4<br>4 Excellent<br>3 Good<br>2 Fair<br>1 Poor | Room for improvement |
|---|---|---|---|
| ORGANIZATION | I planned and researched my topic well. | | |
| PRESENTATION SKILLS | I incorporated tips from the Presentation Skill box in my preparation. | | |
| FLOW OF IDEAS | My ideas flowed logically, and I stayed on topic. | | |
| PREPAREDNESS | I was well prepared. It was obvious I had practiced enough. | | |
| DELIVERY | I spoke clearly and loudly enough so everyone could easily understand me. | | |
| BODY LANGUAGE | I held the audience's attention with varied gestures and eye contact. | | |
| CONFIDENCE | I was relaxed and spoke with ease and enthusiasm. | | |
| VISUAL AIDS | I incorporated visual aids and used them effectively. | | |
| TIME | I spoke within the two-minute time frame. | | |
| RESPONSE TO AUDIENCE | I was able to effectively answer questions and respond to comments. | | |

## StartUp Level 6 SB Photo Credits

### Cover

Ezra Bailey/The Image Bank/Getty Images (front); Tovovan/Shutterstock (back).

### To the Teacher

Page ix (Oscar Blanco): Pearson Education Inc.; ix (Oscar Blanco and Hana Lee): Pearson Education Inc.; ix (friends): YinYang/E+/Getty Images; ix (p. 5 bottom, right): Pearson Education Inc.; ix (photo from MEL): Pearson Education Inc.; ix (bottom): G-stockstudio/Shutterstock.

### Welcome Unit

Page 2 (1): Shutterstock; 2 (2): Shutterstock; 2 (3): DGLimages/Shutterstock; 2 (4): Undrey/Shutterstock; 2 (5): Barock/Shutterstock; 2 (6): Air Images/Shutterstock; 3: Ezra Bailey/The Image Bank/Getty Images; 4: Pearson Education Inc.

### Unit 1

Page 5: YinYang/E+/Getty Images; 5 (Oscar Blanco): Pearson Education Inc.; 6: Pearson Education Inc.; 7: Pearson Education Inc.; 8 (Oscar Blanco): Pearson Education Inc.; 8 (Titanic): Trademark & Copyright © 20th Century Fox Film Corp. All rights reserved. Courtesy Everett Collection; 9: Pearson Education Inc.; 10 (Oscar Blanco): Pearson Education Inc.; 10 (Friends): Arno Images/Cultura/Getty Images; 11: Pearson Education Inc.; 12 (Oscar Blanco): Pearson Education Inc.; 12 (Raymond): Courtesy Everett Collection; 13: Serhii Bobyk/Shutterstock; 14 (Oscar Blanco): Pearson Education Inc.; 16: Vhpfoto/Shutterstock.

### Unit 2

Page 17: Fotoinfot/Shutterstock; 17 (Pablo Pineda): Pearson Education Inc.; 18: Pearson Education Inc.; 19: Pearson Education Inc.; 20: Pearson Education Inc.; 21: Pearson Education Inc.; 22: Pearson Education Inc.; 23: Pearson Education Inc.; 24 (Pablo Pineda): Pearson Education Inc.; 24 (center, right): Africa Studio/Shutterstock; 25: Dragon Images/Shutterstock; 26: Pearson Education Inc.; 28: Gstockstudio/123RF.

### Unit 3

Page 29: Steve Debenport/E+/Getty Images; 29 (Gina Clark): Pearson Education Inc.; 30: Pearson Education Inc.; 31: Pearson Education Inc.; 32: Pearson Education Inc.; 33: Pearson Education Inc.; 34: Pearson Education Inc.; 35: Pearson Education Inc.; 36 (Gina Clark): Pearson Education Inc.; 36 (bottom): Mark Large/Daily Mail/Shutterstock; 38: Pearson Education Inc.; 40: Oko Laa/Shutterstock.

### Unit 4

Page 41: Hero Images/Getty Images; 41 (Oscar Blanco): Pearson Education Inc.; 42: Pearson Education Inc.; 43: Pearson Education Inc.; 44 (Oscar Blanco): Pearson Education Inc.; 44 (hot spring): Teerasak Khunrach/Shutterstock; 44 (bike): Westend61 - Michael Reusse/Brand X Pictures/Getty Images; 44 (raft): Ammit Jack/Shutterstock; 44 (paddleboard): SolStock/E+/Getty Images; 44 (zip line): Tong_stocker/Shutterstock; 44 (snorkel): Stockphoto-graf/Shutterstock; 44 (horse ride): Axel Bernstorff/Image Source/Getty Images; 44 (tour boat): B. Melo/Shutterstock; 45: Pearson Education Inc.; 46: Pearson Education Inc.; 47: Pearson Education Inc.; 48 (Oscar Blanco): Pearson Education Inc.; 48 (hikers): Galyna Andrushko/Shutterstock; 48 (South America): Sonderegger Christof/Prisma by Dukas Presseagentur GmbH/Alamy Stock Photo; 48 (Azure Lake): Kavram/Shutterstock; 50 (Oscar Blanco): Pearson Education Inc.; 50 (fracking background): Trueffelpix/Shutterstock; 52: Efired/123RF.

### Unit 5

Page 53: BraunS/E+/Getty Images; 53 (Michael Stewart): Pearson Education Inc.; 54: Pearson Education Inc.; 55: Pearson Education Inc.; 56: Pearson Education Inc.; 57: Pearson Education Inc.; 58: Pearson Education Inc.; 59: Pearson Education Inc.; 60 (Michael Stewart): Pearson Education Inc.; 60 (hacker): Elnur/Shutterstock; 61: HunterXt/Shutterstock; 62 (Michael Stewart): Pearson Education Inc.; 62 (windsurfer): Maria Nelasova/Shutterstock; 64: Portumen/Shutterstock.

### Unit 6

Page 65: Petekarici/iStock/Getty Images; 65 (Hana Lee): Pearson Education Inc.; 66 (Hana Lee): Pearson Education Inc.; 66 (glass vase): Alexey Kolotvin/123RF; 66 (stone bowl): Dario Lo Presti/Shutterstock; 66 (frame): Piotr Pawinski/123RF; 66 (ceramic): Antonio Veraldi/123RF; 66 (leather case): Praiwun Thungsarn/123RF; 66 (duck): Nadezda/Shutterstock; 66 (vinyl bag): Ogm/123RF; 66 (bookmark): Shane Morris/123RF; 67: Pearson Education Inc.; 68: Pearson Education Inc.; 69: Pearson Education Inc.; 70: Pearson Education Inc.; 71: Pearson Education Inc.; 72 (Hana Lee): Pearson Education Inc.; 72 (Roman soldier): Carlos E. Santa Maria/Shutterstock; 73: Sanneberg/Shutterstock; 74: Pearson Education Inc.; 76: Trebolfotografia/Shutterstock.

### Unit 7

Page 77: NicoElNino/Shutterstock; 77 (Elene Rubio): Pearson Education Inc.; 78: Pearson Education Inc.; 79: Pearson Education Inc.; 80: Pearson Education Inc.; 81: Pearson Education Inc.; 82: Pearson Education Inc.; 83: Pearson Education Inc.; 84 (Elene Rubio): Pearson Education Inc.; 84 (escalator): Marc Bruxelle/Alamy Stock Photo; 84 (cable car): Waldir Bolivar/Shutterstock; 85: Pack-Shot/Shutterstock; 86: Pearson Education Inc.; 88: Pat138241/123RF.

## Unit 8

Page 89: Sunwoo Jung/DigitalVision/Getty Images; 89 (Michael Stewart): Pearson Education Inc.; 90: Pearson Education Inc.; 91: Pearson Education Inc.; 92: Pearson Education Inc.; 93: Pearson Education Inc.; 94: Pearson Education Inc.; 95: Pearson Education Inc.; 96 (Michael Stewart): Pearson Education Inc.; 96 (Asian boy): Srijaroen/Shutterstock; 98 (Michael Stewart): Pearson Education Inc.; 98 (bottom): BGodunoff/Shutterstock; 100: Tom Wang/Shutterstock.

## Unit 9

Page 101: Delmaine Donson/E+/Getty Images; 101 (Hana Lee): Pearson Education Inc.; 102 (Hana Lee): Pearson Education Inc.; 103: Pearson Education Inc.; 104 (Hana Lee): Pearson Education Inc.; 105: Pearson Education Inc.; 106: Pearson Education Inc.; 107: Pearson Education Inc.; 108 (Hana Lee): Pearson Education Inc.; 108 (bottom): Dzianis Apolka/123RF; 110: Pearson Education Inc.; 112: Dinis Tolipov/123RF.

## Unit 10

Page 113: Art Wager/E+/Getty Images; 113 (Oscar Blanco): Pearson Education Inc.; 114 (Oscar Blanco): Pearson Education Inc.; 114 (1): Sherry V Smith/Shutterstock; 114 (2): Taras Verkhovynets/123RF; 114 (3): Dmitry Kalinovsky/123RF; 114 (4): Alkanc/123RF; 114 (5): Farbregas Hareluya/Shutterstock; 114 (6): Benis arapovic/Alamy Stock Photo; 114 (7): Welcomia/Shutterstock; 114 (8): Stepniak/Shutterstock; 115: Pearson Education Inc.; 116: Pearson Education Inc.; 117: Pearson Education Inc.; 118: Pearson Education Inc.; 119: Pearson Education Inc.; 120 (Oscar Blanco): Pearson Education Inc.; 120 (background): Zhukova Valentyna/Shutterstock; 120 (hotel): Aluxum/iStock Unreleased/Getty Images; 121 (background): Zhukova Valentyna/Shutterstock; 121 (hotel): BaLL LunLa/Shutterstock; 122 (Oscar Blanco): Pearson Education Inc.; 122 (background): Minto.ong/Shutterstock; 124: Krugloff/Shutterstock.

## Grammar Practice/Vocabulary Practice

Page 125: Paul Bradbury/OJO Images/Getty Images; 131: ALPA PROD/Shutterstock; 132 (Top): Jan-Otto/E+/Getty Images; 132 (bottom): Dnaveh/Shutterstock; 135: Loocid/Shutterstock; 137: Images By Kenny/Alamy Stock Photo; 140: Patricia Marroquin/Moment Open/Getty Images; 144: LesPalenik/Shutterstock.

## Illustration Credits

418 Neal (KJA Artists), John Goodwin (Eye Candy Illustration), Laszlo Veres (Beehive Illustration)